WALLACE STEVENS:

Merle E. Brown

WALLACE STEVENS:

The Poem as Act

Wayne State University Press · Detroit 1970

Published simultaneously in Canada by
The Copp Clark Publishing Company
517 Wellington Street West, Toronto 2B, Canada.

Library of Congress Catalog Card Number: 72-111042
International Standard Book Number: 0 8143 1427 9

Permission has been granted to quote from:
  Wallace Stevens, *Collected Poems of Wallace Stevens*. New York:
  Alfred A. Knopf, Inc., 1965.
  Merle E. Brown, "A Critical Performance of 'Asides on the Oboe,' " in
  The Journal of Aesthetics and Art Criticism, Fall 1970.

Contents

Preface

The period during which Wallace Stevens wrote his greatest poems was unusually long, extending from 1914, when he was thirty-five, until 1954, when he was seventy-five—and into the year of his death. Of his poems considered as a whole, at least two things can be said with assurance: that there is a certain sameness about them, for Stevens was one who "of repetition is most master"; and that they are extraordinarily rich and diverse. During the thirties and forties, while Stevens was still alive, critics wrote tentatively about his individual poems, opening up this poem and that with a brilliant insight, and largely ignoring the exhaustiveness that comes with saying something about everything. In the fifties and sixties, the opposite was true: with the poet dead, most critics felt obliged to cover the entire corpus of his work and to write definitively about the whole of his career.

Curiously enough, this change in critical approach to Stevens, which seems natural simply in relation to the life and death of the poet, coincides with a basic change in the critical climate of America and England. The New Criticism, which flourished from 1930 to 1950, was oriented toward the individual poem and away from the total career of a poet. The reigning forms of criticism today, the new historicism and various forms of structuralism, have just the opposite orientation. One cannot imagine critics of these schools doing anything comparable to F. R. Leavis's essays on "Ash Wednesday" and "Hugh Selwyn Mauberley" or to R. P. Blackmur's essays on Stevens and Cummings, essays written within a few years of the publication of the poems of which they treat. Contemporary critics seem best prepared to consider poets only after they have died; they aim to place a poet's career within some broader framework, either historical or generic. In harmony with this change, much recent criticism of Stevens has been primarily an act of placement. Thus, J. Hillis Miller and Frank Doggett have viewed Stevens's poetry as framed by a philosophical stance; J. V. Cunningham has summed it all up in the light of stylistic types, and Louis Martz in that of a meditative mode; and Northrop Frye and Joseph Riddel have viewed it from the perspective of Stevens's own poetics.

At the present time the author of one more study of Stevens's poetry faces this dilemma: he would like to respect the sustained character of Stevens's poetry and thus make use of all the recent efforts to sum it up; but, even more, he wishes to do justice to the greatness of individual poems and to the immense variety among those poems, and thus take advantage of such fine criticism as that of Blackmur. The two aspirations, however, seem incompatible. Leo Spitzer wrote brilliantly of individual poems, Georges Poulet of the totality of a poet's work; and each knew his work to be inadequate to the objectives of the other. There was no reconciliation.

I am not so bold as to claim that I have achieved a reconciliation beyond the powers of Spitzer and Poulet; but my aim has been directed toward the general vicinity of such a reconciliation. Within a critical context in which mighty efforts are being made to sum up and place Stevens's career once and for all, I have aimed at revitalizing the sense of the greatness of Stevens's poetry and the sense of the variety of his individual poems. In the first chapter, in presenting a conception of poetry which I feel to be adequate to the greatness of Stevens's poetry, I have set this conception in opposition to that of the New Criticism, not because its critical approach is inadequate to individual poems, but rather because it is more clearly adequate than that of any other form of criticism I know. In an effort to preserve the strengths of the New Criticism but also to liberate myself from its weaknesses, I have sought to set forth a theory of poetry and criticism which would permit me both to account for the sameness of Stevens's poetry and to do justice to the richness and variety of his individual poems.

Although I have a definite ideal of literary criticism, this ideal does not force a single methodology upon the practicing critic. It gives direction, but it also frees the critic to use the most diverse methods according to the differences among the poems which he studies. This ideal is meant to encourage responsiveness to the self-originative nature of each great poem and to the element of contingency between one poem and another. Thus, the different parts of this book have something of an occasional nature about them, echoing Stevens's belief that "The poem is the cry of its occasion." The form of each chapter is developed on the basis of the poems treated within it and in relation to the contemporary state of criticism on those poems. One's criticism should, I agree, be unified, but in such a way as to permit and foster the utmost flexibility. It must allow for the fact that great poems do not fit neatly into a serial career, for the fact that, in a sense, a poet has as many careers as he has great poems, because each of those poems is itself both culminative and originative. Fidelity to the sameness of Stevens's poetry must leave room for the rich

9

diversity of his individual poems. Above all else, one loves individual poems, even though it is also true that he loves those poems as the creations of a single, great poet. The effort to find the real Wallace Stevens as Poet within and behind the many sensuous selves and sensuous worlds that are his poems may be justifiable. But the MacCullough is real only as actualized in MacCullough; the ocean of Stevens's poetry is real only as it breaks into the emeralds which are his individual poems. One's final loyalty is to poems which are the realizations of poetry, not to the poetry which is realized in this poem or that. Unity and method there must be; but they must be anti-methodological. As a poet Stevens was a professional amateur; his critic, I believe, must be one too.

1

Criticism as the Animus of Poetry

I

The poems of Wallace Stevens, like all original poetry, ask much of their critical reader. Not only must he read carefully, but he must put all in question, even the very manner of his reading; and implicit in this requirement is the demand that he reconsider and possibly modify his conception of the nature of poetry and his theory of what the critical reading of poetry can or ought to be. Every critic—and this includes every reader who is conscious of what he is doing—develops his conception of poetry and his theory of literary criticism out of his experience and understanding of the poems he reads. Genuinely new poetry inevitably proves difficult because, in its newness, it cracks the frame and the patterns of the critic's expectations. The poems of Wallace Stevens suffered from weak criticism even more than most poetry, because the criticism whose patterns of expectation they violated was itself, at the very time these poems were first published, in a period of vital, exploratory growth. And in such a period a critical framework is least open to radical modification. Now that the efficacy of the New Criticism has declined, however, it should be possible for us to recognize its limitations, to permit Stevens's poetry to break its patterns, and to affirm and adopt a conception of poetry and a theory of criticism in harmony, rather than at odds, with the distinctive greatness of that poetry.

However lively their practice was, most New Critics quite consistently spoke of the poem as of something finished and thus more like death than life as it is lived in the actual present. What, for instance, could sound more skeletal and inactive than the well-known definition of a work of art as "a whole system of signs, or structure of signs, serving a specific aesthetic purpose"?[1] Although William Empson may avoid the inorganic implications of Wellek's definition when he talks about the way in which a poem ought to be criticized, he makes it sound like an old dog bled dry. In his *Seven Types of Ambiguity,* he has this to say of what critics should do with the poems they read:

> They must have the power first of reacting to a poem sensitively and definitely (one may call that feminine) and then, having fixed the reaction, properly stained, on a slide, they must be able to turn the microscope on to it with a certain indifference and without smudging it with their fingers.[2]

The scientific analogy is only a symptom; the inner weakness is that Empson would not have the critic think about the blood of the poem until it has been extracted and smeared upon a slide.

The reason so many New Critics have petrified poems when they theorized about them is to be found embedded in their peculiar strength, in the fact that most of them were practicing poets and were, as a result, deeply suspicious and fearful of self-consciousness. As poets their fear of self-conscious thought had some foundation; as critics it was disastrous. One might think that poets turned critics, that is, poets thinking about poetry, would have to be self-reflective. This group of poet-critics, however, proved their fear of such reflective thought by almost uniformly refusing to think of themselves as poets even when they thought about the poetry they themselves had made. When they turned upon poetry, either their own or that of others, as an object of thought, they did not think about the act of making a poem. Instead of thinking critically about the way in which poets think and feel poetically, instead of considering the manner in which poets consider things, even as critics they considered only the things which poets consider. They ignored their own poetic eyes and attended only to those things which they had attended to as poets.

The mistake is an old one for poet-critics, and may be found in an early manifesto, the preface to the second edition of the *Lyrical Ballads*. Surely the way in which Wordsworth observes the "violet by a mossy stone" is as important a part of his poem as the violet itself is. But as a critical theorist Wordsworth neglected this fact. When he said, "I have at all times endeavoured to look steadily at my subject," he meant for the critical reader to do the same, that is, to look steadily at his subject and to ignore his act of looking steadily at his subject. Similarly, when New Critics have spoken of a poem as an objective correlative, they have meant that the poem as object, as fact, has taken the place of any feeling, any subjectivity, and any activity which might be constitutive of it. The real poem is an object, the line "Rocks, moss, stonecrop, iron, merds" or the line "With rocks, and stones, and trees," and not an act of self-translation, an action containing a feeling which it is in the process of turning into that line.[3] They have committed the same error as those existentialists who concentrate upon the existence of something and ignore the act of its coming into existence.[4] In their critical thought, they have reduced

13

poetry to an object. Because of the manifestly active nature of the movement of Stevens's poems, their critic has a special obligation to free his idea of poetry from its box, to take the poem as painting off the wall, and to make it actual by the reconstructive power of his imagination.

A poem is not the product of any refining process. It is not analogous to sulphurous acid after the catalytic filament of platinum has worked upon it. For a human being arranged that experiment. If poetry had to be thought of as analogous to a scientific experiment, surely one should not blind himself to the part played in the experiment by the person who arranges it, for the act of arranging is a crucial part of the experiment itself. The analogy, however, should be dropped altogether. A poem is a human act of self-translation, of translating the dark current of feeling into translucent gems. The critic's concern should be not merely with the jewels produced but also with the poetic act of transforming the flow into those jewels, because the poem as action is composed of and originative of both the flow and the jewels as an identity of opposites. To concentrate only upon the product may be good consumer economics, but it is to ignore the forceful current in the process of being transformed. For that matter, it is too little to consider only the fluid force and the carved artifact, for in doing that one is missing the highly complex activity of turning the one into the other. When Ezra Pound says,

> The thing that matters in art is a sort of energy, something more or less like electricity or radioactivity, a force transfusing, welding, and unifying. A force rather like water when it spurts up through very bright sand and sets it in swift motion.[5]

he is evidently recognizing the flow and the product; and he also shows that they go together in his striking image of the bright sand being set in motion by the water. But the act of transformation itself is left most obscure: it is "something more or less like electricity or radioactivity," whatever that analogy may mean. The fact is that Pound is considering seriously only what he felt and thought about when making a poem. He is ignoring his poetic act of thinking; that is, he is refusing to be self-reflective, to be aware of that act of thinking which is the very shaping of the poem, which is, in fact, the poem as an aesthetic experience.

The elemental force and the transforming activity of a poem are just as important to it as are its objectified elements, its meter, rhythm, imagery, characters, themes, and scenes. In fact, these objectified elements can be grasped as poetry only to the extent that they are experienced as the antithetical moment of the poetic act, the thesis being the elemental feeling and the synthesis the overarching act of thinking. The poetic act is an act of self-translation: the poet by his thinking is striving to translate his elemental feeling, his vital force, his inner, most intimate self, into a world of objects, organized rhythmically as expressive of his feeling for life.

Now the impersonal element of the poem does not lie in the poem as a product, a vision, or a world, but rather in the poem as essentially feeling, a vital, flowing force not limited to the finiteness of the poet as one man among many men. Imagine, for a moment, mankind as a giant man, not brittle and morbid like Urizen, but fluid and healthy like Blake's Eternal named Los. In our brokenness, in our finite separateness, each of us is but a point on the skin of this Eternal. An egocentric poet, one who writes in order to assert his own feeling in contrast to that of other human beings, this self-expressive poet will have available for his self-transforming act only the blood flowing from the prick of a finger. His verse will be thin, localized, squeezed. It will be human, to be sure, and thus connected with the vital organ, flowing ultimately from the giant's heart; but it will exclude all that force pumping blood to other areas of the body. In contrast to this, the true poet drives his shaft directly into the heart of mankind

15

itself; he taps its vital source. Or, if that emphasizes his cruelty too much, let us say that his heart, for the duration of the poetic act, dilates to the size of the giant's heart. However large his heart may become, though, in his craft and conventions and in his way of looking at things, the poet must remain his individual, limited self. He may become the MacCullough in the feeling which he would express, he may become the Poetic Angel itself; but as a workman he is only MacCullough, just another human being doing his job like the rest of us. He has, of course, more to work with than most of us. For his job is to translate actively the gigantic flow of feeling into an objectified vision; and it is just there, in his act of translating, that he individualizes the feeling and turns it into a unique shape. With all his critical faculties at work, the poet will ride this barbaric flow into the light of his own experience, translating as much of it as his own manly strength and tenacity and discipline can manage. Or, to shift the image, he will give its savagery his own peculiar ritualistic grace, much as the Pedro Romero of *The Sun Also Rises* forces the bulls he fights to take their place in a ritual shaped by Romero himself.

If it has been necessary to distinguish the impersonality of the poem as act from the older notion of the impersonality of a passive, imitative kind of art, it is even more important to distinguish one's notion of the activity of art from the traditional, Aristotelian notion of artistic action. For Aristotle the act of a tragedy is something objectively separated from those experiencing the tragedy, whether as playwright, actors, or audience. According to my position, however, the poem as an action is not Romero's ritualization of the savagery of the bull as seen from the grandstands; that would involve, as it does for Francis Fergusson in his Aristotelian *The Idea of a Theater*, a passive audience whose only direct relationship to the artistic act is the effect that act has upon it. As I see it, the poem as an act can be experienced only from its own ritual center, a center in which Romero and the bull are one though distinct: the bull as brute feeling, Romero as human intelligence, and the two together as a single artistic act, the savagery being translated into objective grace. Before one becomes an *aficionado* of poetry, he may experience it merely as ritual, or objectified pattern. But to love poetry is to know it as the act of metaphor itself, as the act of translating a savage feeling into a civilized pattern.

If the poet has translated his feeling far enough, a reader can work his way back through its ritualized forms to its savage center, to the most elemental feeling the poet has of life itself. Having arrived at the heart of the poem, at its form-giving, unifying feeling, he can then turn back and see creatively all the objective elements of the poem, as though from the inside out. He will be at one with the poet, seeing the world of the poem with the eyes of the poet, experiencing the poem in that flash of oneness that led Arthur Koestler to describe all genuine poetry as archetypal, and each archetype as an electric shock which lifts the reader out of the ordinary world and into poetic ecstasy. In sum, poetry is not an objective action which can be observed. Even the most acute observer, whose slides are kept free of smudging fingers, will at best miss two-thirds of what is going on. Poetry cannot be observed; it must be participated in. It is a human gesturing, a human body in action, but only as that feels, from the inside, to the actor himself.

A thoughtful reader can actually participate in a poem without the intervention of a miracle. Since the poetic act is carried out by the poet's intelligence, by his sense of how many and exactly which lines are needed to objectify, to realize, to existentialize his feeling, since at every stage he is judging the incompleteness or relative completeness of his translation, since, that is, he is his own critic, his own knower, in the very act of his making, there is no mysterious gap between his activity and that of the critical reader. Just as the poet can make what he makes only if he thinks critically, so the critic

17

can know a poem only if he can make the poem. The principle involved here is that one can make something only if he knows it and one can know something only insofar as he makes it. It is a modern version of Giambattisto Vico's principle, *verum et factum convertuntur,* but with fact changed to act, so that the formula reads: *verum et fieri convertuntur* or *verum est factum quatenus fit,* knowing and making are convertible.[6]

All the critic's preliminary readings, all his philological or scholarly investigations of the poet's life and of the language of his time, all his studies of the objective moment of the poem taken separately, all these have as their immediate purpose a translation in reverse, the carrying of the critic into the subjective moment of the poem so that he can feel the elemental pulse of the poem as act. When that has been accomplished, the critic can proceed to what is criticism proper: a study of the act of the poem itself. He has already studied the world of the poem as it is by itself; and he has experienced the feeling of the poem in its vital flowing forth. He has made his paraphrase and he has had his impression; he has experienced the joy of poetry and he has interpreted lines for what they mean by themselves. He must now explicate the movement of the poem from essence to existence, from feeling to vision. He must gather up the particles of his paraphrase into a critical synthesis in which he shows how the objective parts of the poem contribute to the individual expression of its essential, impersonal feeling. There is no way to prescribe exactly how this should be done. Exhaustive explication is clearly not necessary. A truly critical interpretation of single rhythmic phrases, like Mario Fubini's studies of short passages of the *Divine Comedy* in his *Metrica e poesia,* may convey and clarify much of the fundamental action of a very long poem.[7]

Whatever form it may take, criticism of this sort is the continuation of the translating act of the poem itself. The poem lives only in so far as its nature as fact or as product is being turned into activity or process; it lives, that is, only when it is being heard and interpreted critically. Critical knowing, then, is the existence, it is the perpetuation and the development, of poetic making. Within the poetic act itself, critical activity draws poetic feeling into existence: within the critical act, it perpetuates the poetic act and clarifies it by defining as precisely as possible its dialectical nature, the way in which the poet is translating critically the elemental feeling of the poem into its multiple world. Viewed as an activity, a critical essay must include within it the poem being criticized and must give it a clearer and more intense existence than it has had in any previous critical work. In order to read and understand such an essay, then, one must include within his reading a corresponding reading of the poem of which the essay is the translation.

Integrating poetry and criticism in this intimate way does not mean that they form an identity without significant differences. A poem and a critical essay are essentially different: the essence of a poem, its poetry, is feeling; the essence of critical writing is self-consciousness, is the thinking through of the relationship between the feeling and the world of the poem, is the articulation of the poetic action of the poem, the act of translating its essence into existence. As existent, a poem and a critical essay include the same moments, the subjective moment of feeling, the objective moment of multiplicity, and the overarching moment of self-conscious thinking. But the moment of feeling dominates poetic activity, whereas the moment of self-conscious thinking dominates critical activity. Poetry and criticism form an identity of opposites, but their opposition is not dissolved in their identity.

As identical they form an intimate family, so intimate that they often exist together within the same human body. But as opposites they are antagonistic. Though poetry is the *anima* of criticism and criticism the *animus* of poetry, each is the animus of the other, each is a form hostile to the other. Poetry and criticism are intimately related, but any single act which is one or the other must be essentially only one and not the other. As a result, the gravest danger for whichever activity one is performing is that it slip out of its own essential nature and into that of the other. The sharper a poet is critically, the greater the danger is that the balance of power will shift in his verse from the poetic to the critical principle; and if it does, the center of his action will cease to be feeling and will become self-conscious thinking. The more poetic a critic is, the greater the danger will be that he will lose his critical center and will begin to unify his ideas poetically, by means of feeling. For example, as brilliant as R. P. Blackmur's early essay on Stevens is, his last essay, "The Substance That Prevails," is deeply obscure.[8] At his best, Blackmur is so fine a critic just because he is so intensely at one with the poetry about which he writes. But to remain a genuine critic he must subordinate this lyrical identification with the poetry to his own act of thinking through connections. When the lyric feeling overflows his thought, then his critical judgment is awash. Instead of either great criticism or great prose poetry, one is apt to find that the wavering balance of Blackmur's mind has not been fixed and that he has provided only a broken event composed of two incipient and contradictory attitudes, of two attitudes neither of which he had the strength to turn into an act. The poet must be critical and the critic poetic; but there is a balance for each to maintain against the enticements of the other. By the very nature of things, poets and critics should be wary of each other. The extremely ambiguous attitude toward criticism expressed by that critical poet Pope in his *Essay on Criticism* and analyzed so brilliantly by that poetic critic Empson in his *The Structure of Complex Words* reveals a sure insight shared uneasily by those two poet-critics.[9] Opposition is true friendship.

II

The theory of poetry and criticism being presented here, as a prelude to its actual exercise, involves the supersession of a number of ideas important not only to the New Criticism but also to certain critical positions being developed in its wake. The notion of poetry as autonomous and inviolable, cherished by Murray Krieger as the crowning jewel of the New Criticism and as essential to all criticism, must be modified, if not discarded. Every poetic act, one agrees, is autonomous in the sense that it is not simply derivative from a previous action, but has its own originative source irreducible as an action to a place in any system of laws, however complex. The weakness of the New Critical notion of poetry as autonomous and inviolable, however, is that it allows a human being to enter into a poem only in some inexplicable way; and once in the poem this person cannot act or think as a human being: so that, finally, when he is released from the poem, it is impossible for him to give a description of his poetic experience adequate to "the fullness and the complexity of the internal relations of its unique contextual system."[10] The poem is holy and one enters it by grace. Once outside the temple one could no more speak truthfully about what happened within it than he could give a full and accurate account of a mystical experience.

It might appear that I am simply reversing the relationship between poetry and criticism so that criticism is made to seem holy and poetry humble. But that is not the case. The poet contains within his critical activity a vital, supra-personal feeling and he strives to translate it into an existent world. He is as holy as you wish, in his act of tapping something elemental; but he is also most human, most thoughtful, in the very act of making his poem. Because the poet knows in a human way in the very act of his holy making, the critic has a way into the poem as a human being. He can think critically about a poem without introducing something alien into it. The critic's act of thinking is not a violation of the nature of poetry, as it must be for those who believe in the holy autonomy of poetry. Because a poet can speak poetically only if he listens to himself critically, the critic, whose essential job is to listen critically, need not humiliate himself in order to enter the poem. His main job, even when engaged with the poem, is to be essentially himself. He must, it is true, become something more than a mere critic. For he must split into two *personae,* one his own thoughtful listening and the other the poet's impassioned speaking. Nonetheless, there is nothing mysterious in such an act of splitting oneself into speaker and listener. It is the commonest thing in human experience; it is the heart of all communication. One can speak only if he can hear himself; and one cannot truly listen to the speech of another person except by re-enacting that speech within himself. Human communication is not mysterious simply because it is different from the immediate stimulus and response of two sentient organisms.[11]

Another, even more deeply founded, and intractable idea from which one must be free if he is to appreciate Stevens's poetry is the notion that great poetry is always sensuous, concrete, and even visually imagistic. According to this conception, poetry must be based upon a sense of "this world, this place, the street in which I was." When Randall Jarrell expressed his uneasiness at Stevens's later poetry in this way, "Surely the poet *has* to treat the concrete as primary, as something far more than an instance, a here to be sensed, a member of a laudable category," he meant by primary concreteness just this: the one and only sensuous world in which we all live.[12] With such a notion of poetic concreteness, what could one do with a poet who says:

And out of what one sees and hears and out

22

> Of what one feels, who could have thought to make
> So many selves, so many sensuous worlds,
> As if the air, the mid-day air, was swarming
> With the metaphysical changes that occur,
> Merely in living as and where we live.[13]

Although Louis Martz appreciates Stevens's meditative poetry, at least when it reminds him of the meditative poetry of the seventeenth century, he also reveals his allegiance to this notion in his insistence that such poetry must begin with "the composition of place, seeing the spot," with the use of the image-forming faculty in order to provide a concrete and vivid setting for a meditation on invisible things.[14] The truth is that Stevens's meditations may or may not be sensuously anchored in this way; their quality, most emphatically, does not depend upon their being so.

The ultimate source of this notion is a British fiction, a fiction of British empiricism. The notion is based upon the hypothesis that real experience, that full experience, that all feeling and emotion have an undistorted being only when attached to sensations. The assumption is that experience as given is purely sensory, that true experience can be touched only insofar as we use our senses thoughtlessly, only as we immerse ourselves in the flow of sensations quite innocent of, quite free of, ideas and judgments. It is on the basis of this notion of experience that Alfred Alvarez, as an example chosen from among many, would exalt the poetry of D. H. Lawrence over that of Stevens. Alvarez feels that "Lawrence's gift was to remain continually available to experience. He lacked preconceptions whereas Stevens relied on them." Alvarez's judgment against Stevens is:

> Underneath all his work is an abiding belief in abstraction. His poetic method is controlled by an abstracting principle. . . . It seems as though Stevens was never happy unless he could have all the images and figures

with which his verse abounds tidied away into a framework of decent abstraction.[15]

There is nothing hidden about the adverseness of this judgment. The use of "tidied away" and "decent" means that such
poetry is to be discarded as distasteful. One can imagine what
Alvarez would say of a poem like this:

NO POSSUM, NO SOP, NO TATERS

He is not here, the old sun,
As absent as if we were asleep.

The field is frozen. The leaves are dry.
Bad is final in this light.

In this bleak air the broken stalks
Have arms without hands. They have trunks

Without legs or, for that, without heads.
They have heads in which a captive cry

Is merely the moving of a tongue.
Snow sparkles like eyesight falling to earth,

Like seeing fallen brightly away.
The leaves hop, scraping on the ground.

It is deep January. The sky is hard.
The stalks are firmly rooted in ice.

It is in this solitude, a syllable,
Out of these gawky flitterings,

Intones its single emptiness,
The savagest hollow of winter-sound.

It is here, in this bad, that we reach
The last purity of the knowledge of good.

The crow looks rusty as he rises up.
Bright is the malice in his eye . . .

> One joins him there for company,
> But at a distance, in another tree.[16]

He might admit that Stevens presents a scene of sorts and that the poet even enters the scene at the end. He would, however, add that the voice of the poet and the poet himself are not truly realized in the scene. The poet is so vaguely conceived, he might go on, that Stevens can ungrammatically shift pronouns from "we" to "one" when it comes time for him to join the crow. And, of course, Stevens cannot really be imagining himself in the scene, even at the end, for how absurd the fat man would appear, clawing his way up a tree and then perching there like a vulture. No. The poet remains outside the scene, tossing off odd similes, comparing stalks to crippled human beings and falling snow to eyesight. Even the title, "No Possum, No Sop, No Taters," is a comment on the scene from the outside, an effort to define it abstractly. Finally, Stevens's generalizations, "Bad is final in this light," and "It is here, in this bad, that we reach / The last purity of the knowledge of good," reduce the scene to mere illustration. The life of a generalization is always derivative in genuine poetry, but here it is primary and authoritative.

With a theory of the poem not as organically concrete but as concrescent, as an act translating feeling into an articulated world, under the critical scrutiny of the eye of the poet himself, one can, in contrast to Alvarez, account for the power of the poem. According to this theory, the world of the poet may be as abstract or as concrete, as conceptually thin or as sensually thick as he wishes; for neither kind of world makes a poem or breaks it. The only legitimate question for the critic is whether the multiple elements of the poet's world are being used effectively to translate and bring into existence his elemental feeling. This feeling provides, in its outward reaching and prehensive action, all the sensuousness required of poetry; and its sensuousness may be objectified as fully in abstract

25

ideas as in concrete images. It has to do not with bodies separated from each other and scattered about in an exterior world but with one's own feeling for anything articulate, whether it is his own fleshly body or a body of thought logically integrated. Finally, what gives a poem its immediacy and its concrescence is not its sensations, but rather the overarching act of impassioned thinking, the critical yet poetic act in which the poet strives to shape a world of images or of abstractions or of a combination of images and abstractions which is adequate to the feeling he is trying to draw into existence. Thought, even argument, is as natural to humankind as sensation, and it may show forth and give a shape to feeling as effectively as sensation does.

If "No Possum, No Sop, No Taters" is approached as a poetic act of thinking, its quality as an intensely dramatic poem will become manifest, even though it will still appear to be artificial, lacking organic naturalness. Disjointedness and fragmentation are the most obvious qualities of the poem. Everything is at a distance from everything else; everything curls away in aloofness from everything else. The poet informs us of this in his very title: things are so separated from each other in this world that there is not even the meager unity made possible when poor folk gather around their meal of possum, sop, and taters. Even the form of the title is expressive of distance, for Stevens has chosen his words, "possum," "sop," and "taters" from a world unconnected with any image in the poem proper. Stevens has separated himself, as a maker of titles, from himself as a maker of poems.

The sun's absence from the scene is essential because sunlight unifies any scene that it shines upon; and, as an old sun, it could not give much heat even if it were present. The suggestion that we are asleep, "He is not here, the old sun, /As absent as if we were asleep," prepares one for a scene unrolling darkly before him, as a dream which is observed without participation. The style of the poem is jerky so that even sentences placed beside each other seem to be unrelated:

> The field is frozen. The leaves are dry.
> Bad is final in this light.

From his detached position the observer looks first at one thing, then at another, and then, inconsequentially, makes his pompous judgment: "Bad is final in this light." In lines seven and eight one sentence is repelled by the next by way of direct contradiction; the stalks are said to be without heads, and then they are said to have heads. The comment that the leaves are dry and the observation that they "hop, scraping on the ground" go naturally together, but Stevens has separated them by eight lines unrelated to them.

One is made to feel thankful that he is not included in this scene and to observe it with tender pity. The broken stalk-people are so pathetically helpless that they can articulate their grief only as the fluttering of a tongue. The stupendous image-abstraction of sparkling snow, "Snow sparkles like eye-sight falling to earth, / Like seeing fallen brightly away," bitingly identifies bright, falling snow and the contemptuous repudiation with which thousands of eyes glance sharply at the broken forms and then turn quickly away; and one understands compassionately that social persecution and ostracism are a form of murder. It is only fitting that good people like the observer, looking at this bad scene from the outside, should derive a lesson, good moralist that he is. He can say— and in his wisdom he universalizes his saying, as is his right— that his observations of this badness give him knowledge of its opposite, that is, of himself, of the goodness characteristic of him and of his kind, who, as is clear from the plural pronoun "we," cohere in friendly brotherhood.

This complacency, however, so patent in the claim that "The last purity of the knowledge of good" has been attained, is suddenly upset by that realist the crow. He looks rusty as he rises up because, even in such a world as he occupies, it is rare that he has to deal with any people quite so bad as the observer and his fellows. Nonetheless, he can do his job and teach them a lesson beyond their moralizing simply by looking outside the scene at them with bright malice in his eye. He reminds them of the scorn and contempt of the sparkling snow fallen brightly away, and they know that they have been scorned. Do they receive their epiphany? Maybe not. At this point Stevens is not sure he is in touch with his fellows. But he at least is suddenly illuminated; and, no longer so presumptuous as to identify himself with others, he enters the scene as one alone, sharing at a distance the knowledge of the crow, the knowledge that to look upon suffering from a detached position and to moralize upon that suffering for one's own advantage is, in truth, not pure good, but the purest form of evil. Complacent detachment and pitying condescension contribute to, even create, the very fragmentation observed from their perspective. The poet accepts his shame and plays the fool by climbing a tree and appearing as the vulture he has really been. He is laughable, but those who laugh should not forget the bright malice in the eye of the crow. They remain outside the scene as morally condemned.

Such a reading indicates why the poem cannot be understood if approached as though it ought to have the organic coherence of a picture. The poem is incoherent as an objective world: images and abstractions do not coalesce; rather they repel each other. But they must be this way because of the feeling which the poet is striving to embody in his grotesque world. The movement of his mind as maker of the poem, unlocated in space and time, is what one must experience if he would enter into the feeling of the poem and experience its embarrassing depths. From the organic point of view, even the images of the poem lack concreteness and do not grow together; and the generalizations and the title are, indeed, far distant from the scene of fragmented images. If, however, one accepts the conception of poetic experience as the poet's act of impassioned thinking, every element in the poem is concrete and immediate; it grows together with the poet's act of making a world both abstract and sensory in an effort to express his elemental feeling of brokenness. One determines whether a poem is concrete on the basis of his own conception of living poetic experience. The responsible critic must make sure that his conception of poetic experience is not inferior to that of the poet himself.

III

To appreciate the poems of Stevens, then, one must be free of the notion that, to be genuine poetry, a poem must be a sensuously concrete, autonomous artifact. A final point to be insisted upon is that the poem as act, according to the conception of poetry being presented here, is not a psychic act, is not expressive of the psyche of the poet. My theory is quite distinct from I. A. Richards's idea of the action of a poem as psychic expression, nor does it lend itself to the argument, impressively maintained by Roy Harvey Pearce, that Stevens's poems are egocentric, are expressive of his psychic ego.[17] For Richards, the poem begins, within time, in a state of mind, a complex of attitudes that are, basically, the psyche of the poet. The poet writes a poem to express this psychic state and to communicate it to other psyches. According to my position, in contrast, only the fully realized, dialectical synthesis, which is the action of the poem, achieves existence. No one of the three moments of the synthesis is in itself existent. The thesis of the poem, its basic feeling, even though its very essence, exists only as part of the poem itself. The feeling has existence only as objectified and only as drawn into the world of the poem by means of the action of the poet's thinking. Furthermore, the moments of the poem are not related chronologically; no moment is first, last, or middle, according to any time measurement which one might apply to the poem. If any segment of a poem were extracted from the poem and analyzed, all three moments of the poetic act would be found to be equally present within it. The poem is not the translation of a preexistent feeling into a poetic vision. The poem itself is the translating of feeling into vision and both feeling and vision are included within the act of translating and have their only existence as part of that action.

Even the poetic feeling itself is not psychic, is not to be confused with emotion. It is inclusive of all the psyches as of all the images and objects of the poem and is constitutive of them. Even outside poetry, for that matter, human feelings are not confined to the psyche of the person who experiences them. They are our fundamental, even primitive, way of prehending the world, are a reaching outward, and are as much a part of the objects and outer events of the world to which we attend as they are a part of ourselves. To box feelings within the psyche and to delimit them there is a need of experimental psychology and is legitimate and useful for purposes of quantification. In the world as experienced, however, our feelings suffuse the world, they are the fountains in the sky, they in fact bind us to all we love. Stevens himself was quite aware of this essential aspect of human feeling. In commenting to Hi Simons on the first part of "The Man with the Blue Guitar," he said: "the poet was required to express people beyond themselves, because that is exactly the way they are. Their feelings demonstrate the subtlety of people."[18] The bodiliness of experience, and particularly of poetic experience, is not merely the bodiliness of the individual psyche; it is the bodiliness of the world as experienced by human beings.

As a result of this conviction, common to my conception of poetry and to Stevens, one must be wary of Pearce's notion that Stevens culminates a tradition of egocentric poetry. For the most part, Pearce analyzes egocentric poetry in his *The*

Continuity of American Poetry without stretching the notion of the ego unduly. Traditionally the ego has been thought of as substantial, a self objectified in the world, one self among many selves, one psyche among many. To write what Pearce calls egocentric poetry is to accept the limitedness of one's own point of view as final and to feel that such a limitation is tolerable. One may try to encompass a whole world within his particular perspective; but all that one sees and feels, as poet, he experiences from his limited and definable position within the given world. Clearly this theory of egocentric poetry is a variation on the theory of poetry as sensory and organic. To be either experiential or egocentric, the voice of a poem must be speaking within a given situation which is conditioned by a certain place and a certain time.

The main trouble with such egocentric poetry is that it must be composed in profound ignorance. For, with a little thought, the poet must recognize that, as poet, he is more than the egocentric voice speaking within the given situation of the poem. Obviously enough, the very sense of there being a situation, a place, and a time that condition and limit the voice of the poem is as much the creation of the poet as the voice itself is. In the act of making the poem, the poet contains the situation just as the situation contains the egocentric voice. To have a poetic sense of the limits of one's perspective entails that one have a sense of what is beyond those limits; and, since nothing exists in poetry except that which the poet has a sense of, the poet as maker must extend beyond the limits of any and every voice and perspective that is expressed within the poem. Now, whatever development there may be in Stevens's career as a poet, it is clearly related to an enhancement of his self-awareness.

Thus, it can be no surprise that, at least as early as "The Man with the Blue Guitar," Stevens was striving to overcome his egocentric limitations and was making a distinction between his act of poetic making and himself as ego. At one

31

point in that poem he asserts the position which Pearce finds
to be characteristic of him:

> Tom-tom, c'est moi. The blue guitar
> And I are one[19]

or, my poetic making and I are one. But he at once reacts to
this position with revulsion:

> The pale intrusions into blue
> Are corrupting pallors

that is, the intrusions of my pale egocentrism corrupt the pure
blue air of poetry. He then distinguishes himself as ego, as
animal, from his poetry, from his guitar playing. As a man he
is no more than the ordinary men who would have him "play
things as they are"; he is merely another "lion locked in
stone." As a man caught up in the act of making poetry, however, he is "the lion in the lute." The poetry itself is

> The unspotted imbecile revery,
> The heraldic center of the world
>
> Of blue, blue sleek with a hundred chins,
> The amorist Adjective aflame. . . .

It is pure feeling, pure love, pure pleasure; but it takes on
existence by the act of unfolding into and forming and sur-
rounding the ordinary world of men in their brutishness. Although Stevens's later poetry is often about men as animals,
Stevens the animal, the ego, is striving to be more than a mere
ego; he is striving to be released from his stone encasing and
tranformed into "a lion in the lute," an ordinary ego contained within the poetry itself, within the strumming of the
blue guitar.

Any number of Stevens's later poems develop this sense of

the difference between the ego and the imaginative act of a poem. One's greatest joy is to sense that in his littleness, in his egocentric limitedness, he can be contained by and unified with the godly act of poetry. The sustained feeling of these poems is a unity of humility and exaltation. The man never forgets his littleness, his humble status, even when he feels at one with the transcendental act of the poem; but he also rejoices in that transcendence. In one of his last poems, "Prologues to What Is Possible," for example, Stevens sets forth in the first part "an ease of mind" which is the center of pure poetic making, an act beyond the ordinary world of men as egocentric; and then, in the second part, he shows the limited way in which he as a sensitive individual can participate in that act.[20] Part one presents a state of mind, an ease of mind, something beyond the individual man, a supreme fiction, a creative ease, a comfortable fertility, a feeling both exploratory and secure, a sense of being beyond everything fixed and yet being utterly sure of where one is. Part two shows the individual, the individual animal rather than the poet, as afraid himself of being identical with the pure state of the first part; yet he then proceeds to explore himself hesitantly and finds that at certain moments he does experience an ease of mind both secure and exploratory. His experience is not identical with the sublimity of pure poetic action but rather combines its grandeur with his egoistic littleness.

After the long lines of the first part, which combine colloquial easiness and an almost breathless swiftness, come timid, cumbersome lines, with embarrassed "which" clauses, imageless "thises and thats," and a general sense of lethargy and idleness. But once the egocentric man asks what self may be snarling in him for discovery, he begins his own sweep of discovery, one parallel to the movement of the first part. And the enfleshed, static, hesitant, cumbersome, noun-weighted, action-denying lines of the man fearful of moving beyond his mere ego are released into a limited act of poetic thinking.

Even the animalistic man can move from one discovery to another, dampening, however, the exaltation of pure poetry, because of the unavoidable limitations of his ego. Thus, he sees not with a speculum of fire but only with "the smallest lamp"; and though its capacity to reveal is puissant, it works only in a flickering way. Its flicks, though slight, reveal magnitudes: as a single light creates a universe, as a first thing adds to a whole vocabulary, as a mere touch reveals magnitudes. In sum, in this poem as in so many others, Stevens presents his finite, egocentric self, but only as caught up in the transcending act of poetic thinking.

Stevens's later poems both affirm and realize the belief that to the extent that we as men participate in genuine poetry of exploration and discovery, to the extent that we overcome the limits of time and space and sensations and organisms, we rise to a oneness with the supreme fiction of creativity and knowledge. Then, and only then, may we say, "God and the imagination are one. . . ." Then and only then can we sense the joy of the line "How high that highest candle lights the dark."[21] One surmounts his life as a finite ego, as an object in space and time, only at rare, unpredictable moments. But then at least his life is truly poetic and he is at one with the poetic act of making. Poetry based upon such an awareness cannot be described as egocentric.

It is true that in Stevens's poetry the ego is not annihilated in the act of poetic creation; it is rather engulfed in something vaster than itself. It is also true that the divine act of poetry as one experiences it is tinged by his own limited nature. If one's name is MacCullough, when he rides high in poetry he does not become God directly, he becomes God only as conceived and felt and experienced by himself; that is, he MacCullough becomes the MacCullough. To claim more would be presumptuous. Dante's God is God as experienced by Dante; we know of the mystic intrusions of divinity into Eliot's poetry only as they were experienced by Eliot. Surely this does not make Dante's and Eliot's poetry egocentric. Nor is Wallace Stevens's poetry egocentric, even though he, unlike Dante and Eliot, expresses his awareness that his God is a supreme fiction. One would call it so only because he has a notion of poetic experience more limited than that of the poetry he is interpreting.

New poetry forces new theories of criticism upon us. The most sensitive reading and interpreting of poetry like that of Stevens will obscure and distort the poetry if the critical theory underlying the reading is inadequate. Stevens's poetry forces one to abandon the theory of poetry as organic and as necessarily dependent upon sensations; it requires a theory of poetic experience as an act of thinking, an act in which the poet, self-conscious and world-conscious, draws his feeling into an objective world. This world need not itself be sensuous or visual; it may be abstract, it may even be the profession of a final belief. It need not be the world as given in common experience, or any part of it. It need not be a world viewed from an established point within it. Finally, it need not be an expression issuing from a finite ego. For the act of poetic thinking and making goes beyond one's own ego, one's own point of view. Such thinking, such impassioned and active thinking, is itself the source of that particular space and time or of that abstract world by which the poet strives to express the elemental feeling of his poem.

2

Poems of the Body in *Harmonium*

Not the Poetry or the Poetics of *Harmonium* but its poems
are our concern. Observe how that disturbing "The poem of
the mind in the act of finding / What will suffice" changes,
under the scrutiny of Joseph Riddel, into his own concern,
"The growth and development of what Stevens liked to call
the 'life of the imagination,' as it is recorded in individual
poems and in their relationships."[1] Riddel claims that often
one of Stevens's poems grows out of a previous one and that
his "achievement must be measured in the continuity and development of his work, as it expresses a life lived in the mind,
a life not only recorded but realized in poetry." Especially
after the entire corpus of a poet's work is possessed, the great
temptation is to reduce his poems to something above and
beyond them, to his Poetics and to his Poetry. The needs of
one's own book, the need to make a coherent, unified statement about the whole body of the poet's work, even to the
neglect of the integrity of the individual poems, leads one

to shift his focus from "the poem of the mind in the act" to the development of the mind from poem to poem and beyond all the poems. In Stevens's work, however, the mind in action is bodied forth in poems; between or beneath or beyond these poems, there is no poetic action or mind.

The poet who wrote "Beauty is momentary in the mind, / The fitful tracing of a portal, / But in the flesh it is immortal" and, later, "The greatest poverty is not to live / In a physical world" requires that one concentrate upon his poems as physical acts bodying forth mind.[2] The plausible claim that one should view Stevens's poetry as embodying "typical forms of thought," a claim Riddel shares with Northrop Frye, leads inevitably away from Stevens's greatness. Frye's uprooting and distorting of "Beauty is . . . The fitful tracing of a portal" and neglect of "Beauty is momentary in the mind . . . / But in the flesh it is immortal" should caution one that possibly both he and Riddel are misrepresenting the meaning of "The poem of the mind in the act" so that it tells less of Stevens's poems than of the abstractive, generalizing, non-physical nature of their own type of thought about Stevens.[3]

The greatness of Stevens's poems is that they are all body, that each is a bodying forth, a movement from elemental feeling outward into every cell of a fully formed body, a body felt inwardly as the fingers with which one grips a pen, not as fingers gripping a pen as observed from the outside. Unlike the careers of Wordsworth or Goethe, Stevens's cannot be tapped if one slights his poems in pursuit of his life or theory of the mind. *The Necessary Angel,* and even more the *Letters,* convince us that the poetic life of Wallace Stevens is embodied in his poems, and only there. From the shame he felt at having broached the subject of death at a party given by Harriet Monroe, it is evident that Stevens learned the difference between the poem as a social act and social engagements.[4]

The poems of *Harmonium* require a criticism that is indi-

37

vidualizing rather than generalizing. These poems bear witness against our habits of either soaring swiftly, eaglelike, toward summary generalization or remaining heavily grounded in the sensual sounds of the poem. Once, books were written about Tennyson and Leopardi as philosophers; now reciters of poetry swarm over our college campuses. Everything in Stevens cries out against such misuses of his poems. The criticism needed for Stevens, now and always, is analogous to the performing arts. This criticism is like the performance of a play. Like a producer and his actors, the critic must reconstruct a given text imaginatively in such a way as to perform it. Like a concert pianist, he must turn a text or score from object into beautiful movement, from fact to act, from mere mind or mere body into its irregular, sensual metaphysics, as Blackmur would have said. The reciter of poems is less like a performing artist than like a stereophonic record player in his sense that mere bodily presence, louder and louder, more and more mindless body, is true performance. In poetic recitation there is simply nothing analogous to the arduous technical training and that leap from technical excellence to truly artistic performance that are characteristic of the performing arts. There is no true art of poetic recitation. In itself it gives only the physics of a poem; it moves toward artistry only as it ceases to be itself; only as it becomes either an actual making of the poem on the spot (as in Lord's singers of tales) or a critical reading which includes mere recitation as but one of its subordinate parts.

In protecting himself against perversion, however, the critic will no doubt be less wary of recitation than of interpretation. Even at its best, interpretation, like that of Northrop Frye and Frank Doggett, like that advocated by E. D. Hirsch, Jr., in his *Validity in Interpretation,* tends to reduce poems to prose statements. If the style of a poem were distinct from its content, then meaning could be adequately studied as separate from significance, and fact from value. Indeed, merely lit-

erary works, the products of fancy, can be captured by interpretation, which, essentially, abstracts shared meanings, the
meanings held in common by a poet and his contemporaries.
Interpretation is adequate to all that is unoriginal, uncreative,
and unimaginative. The great poem, however, and there is
no other kind, the poem as synthesis of individual and universal, of signature and archetype, of form and content, style
and meaning, expression and intuition, cannot be caught by
interpretation any better than by recitation. The fact and
value of a poem are inseparable, and critical characterization
and evaluation are contingent upon each other. Any poem, to
be sure, may be interpreted; in a leveling society the charms
of such an approach are enticing. When the wealth of imagination has been reduced to the poverty of fancy, however, the
beneficiaries of their unhappily won equality will cry out
against their "scientific" benefactors. Heightening, not leveling, is imperative for the critic. To take support from a peer
of Stevens, Ramon Fernandez says:

> It seems to me at times that the true masterpieces are
> Phoenixes which need a reader's attention each time
> they are to be reborn. The others, to the contrary, the
> wretched books, call out imperiously to you . . . Time,
> ease of mind and energy are required to revive a true
> masterpiece, for to be such it must bring together all
> of its author's most intimate and passionate feelings. A
> masterpiece will reveal itself only to one who, because he
> knows how to read it, already merits its complicity. It
> is the least democratic of human productions.[5]

II

A poem in *Harmonium* is not the sufficiency of the fact of
a mental discovery. It is an action, not resolving itself into
a proposition; and the critic's job is to protect its violable
nature from such destructive resolutions. Here, for example,

is a product of fancy. "A Soldier" by Robert Frost is comparable to Stevens's "The Death of a Soldier" not only because
of subject matter but also because both pieces depend on a
double movement, Frost's on the arc of the lance and the arc
of the spirit, Stevens's on the wind that stops with the soldier's
death and the wind that continues to move the clouds over
the heavens (incidentally, the comparison is not meant to set
Stevens against Frost, because "A Soldier" is not one of Frost's
finer poems, whereas "The Death of a Soldier" is one of
Stevens's).

A SOLDIER

He is that fallen lance that lies as hurled,
That lies unlifted now, come dew, come rust,
But still lies pointed as it plowed the dust.
If we who sight along it round the world,
See nothing worthy to have been its mark,
It is because like men we look too near,
Forgetting that as fitted to the sphere,
Our missiles always make too short an arc.
They fall, they rip the grass, they intersect
The curve of earth, and striking, break their own;
They make us cringe for metal-point on stone.
But this we know, the obstacle that checked
And tripped the body, shot the spirit on
Further than target ever showed or shone.[6]

Frost's mental control is propositional, the sort of control for
which Yvor Winters once praised T. Sturge Moore. If one
tries to perform it, to reenact it, he finds it to be hollow, a pious commonplace decked out in a cliché ("as it plowed the
dust"), a feeble echo of Omar Khayam ("But this we know"),
a cute repetition ("come dew, come rust"), words as frivolous
filler ("ever showed or shone"), and the thud of a lifeless
metaphor ("He is that fallen lance"). There is no pressure of
person on muscle; the lines are mask without substance, tech-

nique without performance, not even body, because not bodying forth mind. In contrast, here is a poem in which spirit is enfleshed:

THE DEATH OF A SOLDIER

Life contracts and death is expected,
As in a season of autumn.
The soldier falls.

He does not become a three-days personage,
Imposing his separation,
Calling for pomp.

Death is absolute and without memorial,
As in a season of autumn,
When the wind stops,

When the wind stops and, over the heavens,
The clouds go, nevertheless,
In their direction.[7]

Stevens's poem is a catch of breath perfectly bodying forth an austere awe before a moment of death without masquerade. The bodily act of mind is itself sufficient in giving value to the appalling, silent, breathtaking acceptance of mortality. One must, as critic, spin away and around and back to these stunning lines, never wrapping them up in an anesthetizing formula, drawing analogies which, in their very inadequacy, propel one back to the sufficing act of the poem, which continues to turn and spin, even if in crystal, in the permanence of infuriated words.

Not, of course, that this action is unrelated to experience other than itself. It is not dependent upon such experience, but, out of its own creative fount, the poem prehends, transforms, intensifies, and deepens that experience each of us has had of the waste and emptiness of the death of a close friend

41

in one or another of the mass wars of our century. Who could have thought that any poet would find a way to redeem such death? Poetic redemption of a death is imagining it as the culmination of a life lived, is to see through it to that harmony wherein the death does not violate the essential nature of the life. The candor and unpretentiousness, the honesty and simplicity and openness of a humble people, so apparent in their rough, unshaped, indelicate lives, are discovered in the austerity of "The Death of a Soldier." The rightness of this death stems from the way one's very breath is implicated in the lines,

> When the wind stops,

> When the wind stops and, over the heavens,
> The clouds go, nevertheless,
> In their direction.

as it is not in this more desolate but less awesome and harrowing poem by Giuseppe Ungaretti:

SOLDATI

> Si sta come
> d' autunno
> sugli alberi
> le foglie[8]

The heroic deaths in Shakespeare's plays, matching as they do the lives of his heroes, have helped men die with a heroic sense of themselves; this death of Stevens aids one in dying humbly. One need not die like "a dog, a horse, a rat," even if also unlike a hero. Only, indeed, if one senses that he can die meaningfully, is it possible for him to live, if not fearlessly, then at least courageously, even in the midst of fear.

What amazes one most in the act of an early poem by

Stevens is its power of propelling him beyond it and then hooking his fleeing mind and compelling it to pass through it and beyond it again and again. Probably every poem does something like this, but few with such urgency as Stevens's. This happens as the very movement of the lines achieves significance and contributes to the poetic, in contrast to the interpretable, meaning. Of "Domination of Black" Stevens wrote:

> I am sorry that a poem of this sort has to contain any ideas at all, because its sole purpose is to fill the mind with the images and sounds that it contains. A mind that examines such a poem for its prose contents gets absolutely nothing from it. You are supposed to get heavens full of the colors and full of the sounds, and you are supposed to feel as you would feel if you actually got all this.[9]

The experience, as Stevens points out, is passive. "At night, by the fire" suggests a relaxed body, conducive to idle revery.[10] Image follows image, but poetically, dazzlingly, with the connections impressively coherent in feeling. What begins complacently gains momentum and then reaches a pitch of intensity at the end of the second stanza with "Full of the cry of the peacocks? / Or was it a cry against the hemlocks?" Not idly but for relief from this fiery intensity, the mind turns to look out the window, at the wind; but its associational momentum is too great and sweeps away the momentary relief with planets turning like leaves, both of which are like the movement of the colors of the peacocks flying down from the hemlocks, all of which are in turn like the movement of flames turning in the fire. Finally, all these brilliant movements are like the movement of darkness, the striding of the color of the heavy hemlocks, the coming of night, so that if the peacocks-leaves-flames-planets protest against the hemlocks-darkness-night-blackness which dominates them, they are really cry-ing out against themselves. At the end, moreover, this tour de force of resemblance is enflamed and illuminated by mind. Between the "heavy hemlocks" and "the cry of the peacocks" this time, and only this time, comes "I felt afraid. / And I remembered. . . ." At last one understands the flashy movement and flood of colors. The vain cry of the peacocks is a cry of fear, and its creative splash is itself destructive. The very idle, brilliant display of the poet, the movement of the poem itself, is destructive. The mind, not nature, cannot endure a vacuum, and such a vacuum is closest when one is idle; so, in fear of death, even as a cry against death, one thinks of image after image. Because one is a poet, moreover, the associations of images are dominated by an inner sense of cosmic oneness. By the end of the poem, the oneness of creation and destruction, of vain display and of fear of death, of the brilliance of leaves and their death and fall, of the display of flames as they disappear, all these identities fold out upon the encompassing movement of the poetic mind which is the poem, a flood of colors, joyous, created straight out of a fear of death and, by its expense of energy, as suicidal as the flames of the "loud fire." Henry W. Wells has sensed the quality of this poem as no one else has. He says, "The imagery is something of a *tour de force,* the lines plotted almost too consciously, the whole a bit too choreographic—with the probable exception of the last eight lines, a calculated climax pulling all parts tightly together."[11] Wells misses only one thing, the thing that makes it a great poem, not a contrivance, the fact that it is the neck of the poet which is wrung by that tight pulling together. The sense of conscious display is the heart of the poem; only if responsive to such vanity can one understand the line "I felt afraid," because the fear, finally and most immediately, is in response not so much to a darkness moving in upon one, as to the destructive blackness characteristic of one's own brilliant display of plotted sounds and colors in this very poem. The movement from idle vanity to crushing discovery is not, to be sure, the poet's stated purpose. But a poet cannot, finally, be his own critic. It is more than enough that he warns against separating the meaning and style of the poem. Once one has separated them, even if consistently speaking of both the meaning and style, he is not truly speaking of the poem.

Are we, in spite of ourselves, moving toward a *Harmonium* genre, the poem of the mind in bodily action, the species of which are various types or forms of thought? I do not believe so. Like every work of art, the genuine poems of *Harmonium* achieve aesthetic form: they are an elemental feeling breaking into articulation under the equilibrating eye of the poet; they are the sea breaking into jewels under the splendid light of the sun. Further, unlike later poems by Stevens, the jewels are not so clearly translucent, and dark waves of passion reach out to engulf the fiery, energetic sun. Even these elementary distinctions, however, have as their scope a critical realization of individual poems. The poems of *Harmonium* are peculiarly discrete. It is as if each poem were a person with a character and personality of its own. It is old-fashioned and wrong to insist that one can speak of a poem only as a type, that the critic can speak of it only by way of a type which may have more than one instance. The uniqueness of a poem is like that of a person; it is understood by repetition, by repeated encounters. The movement of "Domination of Black" develops with one's rereadings; with each new reading more of its distinctive qualities become apparent until the critic re-enacts it in its wholeness and utter uniqueness. Then he begins the arduous action of using words, each of which is abstract and typical, and in itself inadequate, until he writes out and acts out a critical statement which is itself a unique whole that breaks open and illuminates the poem as an individual experience.

The individuality of these poem-persons, furthermore, is that they split internally into various *personae,* all held together by the dominant feeling that is the personal nature of the poem. One cannot seriously conceive of a "poetic mind," belonging to Wallace Stevens, which transcends this person and makes implicit judgments and comments upon it. Stevens's muse, his god, is immanent; in each poem the *vis naturae,* the universal force, takes on an absolutely individualized body. Nor is the action of the poem to be confused with Aristotelian action. For action here is always the container, never the contained; the action does not occur in a scene or context, but rather creates and encompasses its scene and context.

"On the Manner of Addressing Clouds" requires criticism based upon the notion that the poem is a person constituted of dramatic personae, speaking forth and acting as a unified community.

> Gloomy grammarians in golden gowns,
> Meekly you keep the mortal rendezvous,
> Eliciting the still sustaining pomps
> Of speech which are like music so profound
> They seem an exaltation without sound.
> Funest philosophers and ponderers,
> Their evocations are the speech of clouds.
> So speech of your processionals returns
> In the casual evocations of your tread
> Across the stale, mysterious seasons. These
> Are the music of meet resignation; these
> The responsive, still sustaining pomps for you
> To magnify, if in that drifting waste
> You are to be accompanied by more
> Than mute bare splendors of the sun and moon.[12]

Blackmur's comments on the poem are helpful; one's initial response is wonder at the delicate, soundless profundity of the words.[13] If one, however, takes the poem off the page and lives it, the poem turns into a speaker who addresses one group first, the cloud-grammarians, and then turns to speak about

46

the cloudy grammarians to philosophers. (The fact that students rarely take a poem off the page, that there is a taboo against memorization, is a dire sign of our bodilessness, of our uninterest in embodiment, of our tendency to become elongated and to live just a little off the ground, drifting ever so slightly toward the "mute bare splendors of the sun and moon.") Obviously the shifts in pronouns from "Meekly you keep the mortal rendezvous" to "Their evocations are the speech of clouds" and then to "So speech of your processionals returns" mean something. With Blackmur in the lead, however, many have read the poem as non-dramatic, so that these shifts have not been activated within the poem. If the poem is rhetorical instead of dramatic, then the turn beginning with "Funest philosophers and ponderers, / Their evocations" might be taken as a shift from addressing the grammarians to addressing us readers as "you." Then the phrase "Funest philosophers" would be just another metaphor for clouds, like "Gloomy grammarians." Such a reading protects the mystery of the poem, indeed leaves it impenetrable, since no reader can know what Stevens thought about his readers (which includes us, to whom he never gave a thought). Further, it leaves it thickly muffled, as any language so sloppy as not to distinguish grammar from philosophy must be. Even though an American businessman, Stevens was not such a barbarian; by the age of forty he knew the difference, and the poem is adequate evidence of that fact.

Having evoked, in the first five lines, the puffiness and muffled cloudiness of speech as sound, as music, as feeling, as pure grammar, the poet then turns to the logicians, to those whose interest is in concept rather than word, in what is thought of as permanent, not transient, in syllogism not sentence, and tells them that they proceed, that they are articulated, by the movement of speech and thus should not be disdainful of language. Unless they are content with abstractedness, with being non-physical people, with thinking "hard in the dark

47

cuffs / Of voluminous cloaks," unless they would be content with the "mute bare splendors of the sun and moon," they should magnify the meek and gloomy grammarians. Indeed, they do so even if unawares since the grammarians' gowns can be "golden" only if gilded by sun or moon. But Stevens gives them a reason for their act of magnification. The meekness of the cloudy grammarians is really their genuineness, their accepting and expressing the unavoidable transiency of human experience. Their meekness is the meeting point of that "drifting waste," the mere bodily flux of experience, mere recitation, and "the mute bare splendors" of our elemental concepts, mere ascetic interpretation.

That the muffled music of this poem is indeed illuminated by the splendors of thought, that its body is "the mind in the act" is, to be sure, open to doubt; and if the light dispersed the clouds, one would choose against the light and for funest clouds. Poetic understanding, however, never involves such a choice. Its choices are always of inclusion, not exclusion. Poetic negations, as Empson should have convinced all, are imaginatively present. If the light dispels the gloomy mystery, one is not reading poetically; he is turning drama into rhetoric or breaking symbol into image and idea. The dominance of tonal quality in the poem (its alliteration, assonance, consonance, and rhyme) are Stevens's own magnifying of grammar, but not at the expense of philosophy.

III

Precise thought makes its affirmations by way of negation; to think precisely, one must negate the thought that is best and closest to his own. So no one can now write of Stevens without recognizing the fineness of Joseph Riddel's thought by means of negating it. To understand thought, furthermore, one needs to study its context, the matrix of negation out of which its affirmations are made. Poems, in contrast, contain their

own negations and in this way achieve autonomy and snap
their bonds with their ambience, social, intellectual, and even
poetic. They do this most obviously by means of meter, which
is the negation contained within the poetic rhythm of a poem.

No poem illustrates this elemental principle more finely
than "Stars at Tallapoosa."

> The lines are straight and swift between the stars.
> The night is not the cradle that they cry,
> The criers, undulating the deep-oceaned phrase.
> The lines are much too dark and much too sharp.
>
> The mind herein attains simplicity.
> There is no moon, on single, silvered leaf.
> The body is no body to be seen
> But is an eye that studies its black lid.
>
> Let these be your delight, secretive hunter,
> Wading the sea-lines, moist and ever-mingling,
> Mounting the earth-lines, long and lax, lethargic.
> These lines are swift and fall without diverging.
>
> The melon-flower nor dew nor web of either
> Is like to these. But in yourself is like:
> A sheaf of brilliant arrows flying straight,
> Flying and falling straightway for their pleasure,
>
> Their pleasure that is all bright-edged and cold;
> Or, if not arrows, then the nimblest motions,
> Making recoveries of young nakedness
> And the lost vehemence the midnights hold.[14]

The inner, driving, containing action of the poem is a sense
of delight in simple, keen, pure, and nimble connectings, in
the very keenest thinking. Strain is introduced into the feeling,
so that it is made an aspiration not a possession, an action not
a fact, by the inertia of the body, by its drag toward sluggish-
ness, once one's first innocence and vehemence are lost. Even
the title implies this strain between the clean, clipped "Stars

49

at" and the thick-lipped and thick-tongued "Tallapoosa." The entire poem, indeed, is composed of similar opposites, the straight and swift lines so keen as to be dark, the lines between stars, and the moist and mingling and heavy and soft and slushy lines of earth and water. The poem is triumphant, however, because the voluptuousness is presented as emphatically negated: "The night is not the cradle," "There is no moon," "The body is no body," "The melon-flower nor dew nor web." The triumph, moreover, is not merely in a sustained tenseness between affirmed keenness and denied slackness; for the last six lines affirm a synthesis of ascetic keenness and the passion and sensuality denied up to this point. The keenness is present in the arrows flying straight and in the bright-edged pleasure; but something else enters, a passion, a sensuality, electric in its freshness and innocence and vehemence. The sluggardly body is redeemed and young nakedness recovered because of the luminous mind making its keen distinctions. The separateness of keen, straight lines and moist and lax lines in the third stanza is overcome; the keen lines are enfleshed and impassioned and the lethargic lines regain vehemence; the two are one in this triumph of the aging man over his sagging body.

Even the rhythm of the poem, pulsing out its precise music against the iambic meter, bodies forth this triumphant synthesis of tautness and slackness. Scansion is inadequate to poetic rhythm. Rhythm is not variations on meter; it is the living negation of meter. But one captures rhythm, even when unaware of the idioms of the time of the poem, because the negated meter is ever present. The iambic pentameter of the first line of the poem, "The lines are straight and swift between the stars," is negated by the heaviness of the accented syllables and the lightness of the unaccented ones. The meter, that is, is negated by the sharpness of the contrast between accent and its absence. By way of this line, one is prepared to read "The night is not the cradle that they cry" in a manner required not by meter but by rhythm, with emphatic accents on such weak and undistinguished words as "not" and "that" and with no accent at all on the word "they." The "they," of course, in the country of Whitman, are too well known to need an antecedent, "The criers, undulating the deep-oceaned phrase." This third line is noticeably the opposite in rhythm of the first two and the fourth lines of the first stanza. The distinction between accent and its absence is blurred, and a rocking motion is set up by shifts in the position of accented syllables and by the two extra unaccented syllables. The watery slushiness of the line is then accentuated as denied by the sharp beat of the fourth line, and we are prepared for the triumph of the mind over aging flesh.

Throughout the second, third, and fourth stanzas, affirmation of keenness is presented with a strict no accent-accent beat, whereas the dullness denied thumps out in rocking rhythms or in falling rhythms. In the last stanza, however, the two contrasted kinds of rhythm merge, the sense of a metrical foot is buried, and one can only affirm that what will suffice has been found in a voluptuous intensity. The meter is there, working negatively, buoying up and defining the extreme delicacy of the ecstatic dance of time, as age recovers young nakedness, in the only way open to it. But to think of the rhythm as mere variations on meter would distort and weaken one's sense of the rhythmic irregularity of the stanza. The poem is a living person, autonomous, there to be recreated and heard because Stevens had so passionate an ear with which to hear and direct his tongue.

It might seem that such attentiveness to individual and imitative form (to use Yvor Winters's term) must entail overreading, so that no poem need be admitted as a failure. Does not a pianist conceal weak passages by his own exuberance? Will not the critic as performer turn even flat passages into an agile dance of words? What else can follow, if each poem is treated as a unique, formal action? In truth, a good pianist does not conceal weaknesses; the fineness of great music is revealed only if he is genuine. In fact, only in performance, only in the living bodying forth of a poem can its hollow spots be felt and exposed. Only, for example, as one transforms "Le Monocle de Mon Oncle" from an artifact of choice words into a personal act of living rhythm is its fundamental inadequacy recognized. One could guess at its weakness from the fact that the seven stanzas of bitter struggle followed by five stanzas of hilarious jubilance on the part of Stevens's uncle have been compared to the timid turnings of J. Alfred Prufrock by so sensitive a reader as Joseph Riddel.[15] Clearly something in the poem lacks body or some part of its body lacks mind or spirit. But only a performance of the poem delimits its weakness.

The poem does have an action of its own, a dominating, overarching action. It can be said, however, to have merely an "inner dialectic" and no dominant feeling or feeling forth, because its action is not poetically realized. The first seven stanzas may be summed up with these lines of Yeats:

> Bodily decrepitude is wisdom; young
> We loved each other and were ignorant.

The two states of youth and age are set against each other as irreconcilable opposites. The aging speaker is contemptuous of his beloved for not accepting the opposition and for making "believe a starry *connaissance*," even at the age of forty. Since he looks with only one eye, first at youth and then at age, he can see no way to relate them. The one is love, beauty, madness; the other is tedium, ugliness, and wisdom. The fools do not know what is in store for them and they are absurd; the wise know what they are and they are pathetic. In the eighth stanza, however, the poet is obviously celebrating what he calls "The faith of forty." How can this be? How did he escape from his violent bitterness into grotesque comedy?

The change, the nub of the whole poem of one hundred and thirty-two lines, is the last two lines of stanza VII and the first two of VIII:

> Suppose these couriers brought amid their train
> A damsel heightened by eternal bloom.
>
> Like a dull scholar, I behold, in love,
> An ancient aspect touching a new mind.[16]

The importance of the lines is evident from their central position, from the way Blackmur so often returns to them, and, mainly, from one's own sense of the movement and force of the poem. Further, one knows what the lines mean, because of Stevens's comment on them in a letter and because of similar passages which work poetically in other poems, most notably in the much later "Esthétique du Mal."[17] In these lines the poet-uncle is thrust by supposal out of time, out of the two imaginable states of existence, the state of furious love and that of bored wisdom, which he sees as separate because he is looking through his monocle. From the perspective of the laughing sky, from the tip of that gigantic tree, from the unreal, hypothetical, still point of living, laughing wisdom, he can look down upon youth and age as organically related, and can accept his aged loved one and himself as the natural fruit of young love, as warty squashes "Washed into rinds by rotting winter rains." He can even feel superior to fiery youth because, along with his laughing wisdom, he has a vivid memory of his youthful passion. Thus, he can say climactically:

> Last night, we sat beside a pool of pink,
> Clippered with lilies scudding the bright chromes,
> Keen to the point of starlight, while a frog
> Boomed from his very belly odious chords.

In stanza two he spoke with bitter contempt to his aging love:

> Yet you persist with anecdotal bliss
> To make believe a starry *connaissance*

whereas here, at the end of the eleventh stanza, he is himself, with joyous acceptance, doing just that, making believe
"a starry *connaissance*." The crucial difference, evidently, is
that he is aware that the scene, with chromes "Keen to the
point of starlight," is a fiction; he does not ignore the facts,
that the beautiful make-believe is being made by two warty
squashes whose fleshly ugliness is epitomized by the frog that
"Boomed from his very belly odious chords." By keen connections, made possible because the supposing poet abstracted
himself from the course of nature, the two lovers have made
"recoveries of young nakedness / And the lost vehemence the
midnights hold." By means of nimble mental motions, the
poet now, but not until now, can know "That fluttering things
have so distinct a shade," that there is indeed a beauty in
dying, even in rotting things. By their minds, by their brilliantly agile imaginations, they are known: Falstaff, the Wife
of Bath, and, most neglected, Chaucer's Reeve, who knew it
all:

> We olde men, I drede, so fare we:
> Til we be roten, kan we not be rype.

By means of his supposing mind Stevens's uncle overcomes his
one-eyed vision and sees the ripeness in rottenness.

The great hymn, however, is not sung. The basic action was
not realized as feeling. The clotted violence of stage one, the
free flowing joy of stage two, are articulated; but the action
which should have dominated both was not realized as poetic
feeling, even though Stevens intended it to be and even though
a pure interpreter might claim that it is in the poem as its
meaning. That action is in the poem as non-poetic meaning,
it is present abstractly as part of the structure, as pointed to

by the four central lines. But poetically it is absent and thus the poem fails, irredeemably.

This failure has its counterparts in the other long poems of *Harmonium,* especially in "The Comedian as the Letter C." In all these poems, knobs and joints of the structure protrude; they have not taken on the flesh of poetic life. Though full of splendid lines, they rest upon a void, on the absence of elemental feeling, which alone gives poetic achievement. Perhaps because of this, they have proved such interesting matter for interpretation and for recitation. Poetically unsound, these poems lend themselves to other kinds of wholes, all non-poetic.

With the exception of "Sunday Morning," the greatness of *Harmonium* is to be found in its short poems. Not until the 1930s does Stevens come close to perfecting more than one long poem. Poetic greatness, however, has little to do with length. These short poems, each a living action, a portrayal of a person in action whose mind becomes flesh through feeling, are as fine poetically as the long poems of Stevens's later years. Surely "The Idea of Order at Key West" is more complicated than "Stars at Tallapoosa." Complexity, however, is not essential to poetic greatness. "Le Monocle de Mon Oncle" is far more complicated than "The Death of a Soldier," but "The Death of a Soldier" is incomparably the greater poem.

IV

Whether a failure or not, "The Comedian as the Letter C" is, like "Le Monocle," too impressive to be dismissed lightly. Its strengths become manifest as soon as one notes that its basic nature lies in the clash between its content, the career of Crispin, and its form and style. Beginning as a dandy and ending as a fatalist, a "magister of a single room" and the father of four daughters, Crispin goes through a career of elaborate transformations. The style of the poem, however, is unvarying, a fact referred to by others as a serious weakness in the poem.

The strength of the poem arises out of this apparent weakness, out of this dissonance between a developing content and an inflexible style.

Although inflexibility of style may be a flaw, it need not be. In the short "Cortège for Rosenbloom," for instance, Stevens uses a most simple, unvarying style to achieve an absolutely hilarious poem, and he does so even though the style is a judgmental imposition upon the figures who carry out their pious folly within the poem.[18] "Frogs Eat Butterflies. Snakes Eat Frogs. Hogs Eat Snakes. Men Eat Hogs" is a similar, though more complicated achievement.[19] The subject is a man who lives an arid life. The style is the opposite of arid; it is based upon sucking and feeding sounds. "The rivers went nosing like swine," the rivers are time, time sucks up the man's arid life and carries it to death, "seaward to the seamouths." Furthermore, beneath the moist, sucking quality of the style is a somewhat dry, methodical regularity, a click-clack, which is explicitly affirmed in the title. The man at the center of the poem "Knew not the quirks of imagery" and thus is borne off to the sea-mouths unaware, unaware that the butterflies of poetry have their revenge by eating the man stylistically, one of those men who ate the hogs that ate the snakes that ate the frogs that ate the butterflies. So all comes round, as "A man may fish with the worm that hath eat of a king, and eat of the fish that hath fed of that worm." Here, too, then the clash between style and content is the heart of the poem.

It might seem that the style of "The Comedian" cannot be given such significance. In at least two different letters, Stevens emphasizes the importance to the poem of the sounds of the letter *c*, and once he goes so far as to claim that the poem might have gone over better if entitled "The Comedian as the Sounds of the Letter C."[20] Although such talk might indicate a decadent fondness for style to the neglect of imaginative sub-

stance, I take it as a mark of Stevens's reticence, of his unwillingness to impose the magnitude of his poetic undertakings
upon others. Either the poem is imposing on its own or it is
not. In his letters Stevens refuses to do its work for it, though
he gives veiled hints.

Read with attention to the sounds of the letter *c,* "The
Comedian" becomes not only the sounds of the letter *c,* but
also the sounds of the sea itself. Early in the poem, as part of
Crispin's career, he is in fact washed away by the magnitude
of the sea. If one's view is elevated from content to the clash
between content and style, then the whole poem appears as
the experience of Crispin's being washed away by the sealike
style, reappearing, surfacing again and again, only to be del-
uged by hoary belchings. As muffled, cloudy sounds envelop
"On the Manner of Addressing Clouds," so the sealike sounds
of lines like "Ubiquitous concussion, slap and sigh," "Ex-
chequering from piebald fiscs unkeyed," "Stepped in and
dropped the chuckling down his craw," and "So may the relation of each man be clipped," with their "deluging onwardness," engulf the experience of this poem.

The sealike effect of the poem depends not only on these
sounds but also on its rhythm and syntax. Metrically, the
poem is iambic pentameter. Rhythmically, however, it must
be read as four-beat, accentual verse. With alliteration heavier
in this than in any other of his long poems, and with apposi-
tional phrases and parallel clauses rolling by, beyond the
most tolerant expectation, Stevens works for a sealike syncopa-
tion, for a rocking movement cresting with four accents and
troughing with the many unaccented syllables which are consistently failing to emerge as proper iambic pentameter. Crispin is a "nincompated pedagogue," made so by the syncopated
rhythm of the poem. Once caught up in this rhythm, the
reader is swept along from beginning to end with an exhilarating ease:

Except in faint, memorial gesturings,
That were like arms and shoulders in the waves,
Here, something in the rise and fall of wind
That seemed hallucinating horn, and here,
A sunken voice, both of remembering
And of forgetfulness, in alternate strain.[21]

Often the syllable where a fifth accent would come is so weak syntactically that one feels no iambic pull at all. Many times, however, the pull toward iambic pentameter is strong, but it should be resisted because in fact that very resistance is a crucial aspect of the forceful, shouldering, effect of the poem:

The fatalist
Stepped in and dropped the chuckling down his craw,
Without grace or grumble. Score this anecdote
Invented for its pith, not doctrinal
In form though in design, as Crispin willed,
Disguised pronunciamento, summary,
Autumn's compendium, strident in itself
But muted, mused, and perfectly revolved
In those portentous accents, syllables,
And sounds of music coming to accord
Upon his lap, like their inherent sphere,
Seraphic proclamations of the pure
Delivered with a deluging onwardness.[22]

If "down" in the first full line just quoted is read without accent, then the following phrase, "Without grace or grumble," can be read properly with only two accents, while the pull toward a third robs it of its potential gracefulness. Many three syllable words that end lines, like "anecdote" in the second full line quoted, need to be read with an American, heavy accent on the first syllable followed by two unaccented syllables; if this is done, the line ends in a trough, flows smoothly into the next, which begins in the trough and then rises sharply. There are, to be sure, some very long lines requiring five accents, but this should be no surprise since I am not talking about something worked out mechanically; even those lines, in my opinion, sustain the effect of sealike swells and falls.

It has been said more than once that "The Comedian" is Stevens's answer to *The Waste Land*. It is possible. Crane's "Voyages" is Crane's triumphant answer to Eliot's dryness. Crane leaves the "brilliant kids" on shore, to fondle their "shells and sticks, bleached / By time and the elements." Unlike such bright, erudite urchins, for whom the surf seems composed of "fresh ruffles," he knows that as a poet, as an urchin, his true place is "The bottom of the sea," even though it is cruel. So he swims and writes swimmingly. That "The Comedian" made him take the plunge is open to doubt, though his admiration for Stevens is well known. With his delight in puns, Crane might well have noted that the foreign word with which "The Comedian" begins is an ambiguous command, meaning both "take note" and "swim":

> Nota: man is the intelligence of his soil,
> The sovereign ghost. As such, the Socrates
> Of snails, musician of pears, principium
> And lex. Sed quaeritur: is this same wig
> Of things, this nincompated pedagogue,
> Preceptor to the sea? Crispin at sea
> Created, in his day, a touch of doubt.[23]

Had he caught that pun (in a letter to Harriet Monroe, Stevens himself said one of the troubles with writing this long poem is that often he feels like a Guatemalan when he wants to feel like an Italian), he might then have responded to the oceanic rhythm even of the first line, with "soil" bearing its fourth and heaviest accent, and as a result he might have caught its deeper meaning: Swim, man is the intelligence only of his soil, not of the sea, and the sea is where the poet must be.[24] Only there is one something other than a sovereign, Eliotic ghost. Only there can the full body of a poem be born,

59

as the poet, like "Triton incomplicate," shoulders his way in identity with the waves.

Crane went that far himself, whether by way of Stevens or not. It is not so obvious, however, that Stevens made such a voyage in "The Comedian." Exactly where Stevens as poet stands or swims or drowns in this poem is not at all clear. He may, indeed, as many critics have claimed, simply be identifying himself with Crispin, whose size dwindles with the progress of the poem. And he may think of the sealike movement of the poem, which becomes harsher and more mocking as Crispin becomes more trivial, as the impersonal movement of Poetry, unmarked by his own, personal, shaping hand. Throughout *Harmonium* Stevens lacks a sure sense of the poem as a synthesis of the universal and the individual, of the MacCullough and MacCullough. In "The Comedian" there is nothing left of Triton, "Except in faint, memorial gesturings, / That were like arms and shoulders in the waves." In "Tea at the Palaz of Hoon" he tests the idea of the immense, supra-egoistic power of the poet; but it is only a test, touched by an uneasy arrogance suggestive of Stevens's unwillingness to claim so much for the poet. The monotony of the rhythm and style of "The Comedian" has something to do with just this uneasiness; Stevens was not yet ready to take full control of the sea, of the oceanic roll of his lines. What such control involves may be sensed if one turns to the first line of "The Idea of Order at Key West": "She sang beyond the genius of the sea." Even though much shorter, "The Idea of Order," in its exhilarating vastness, makes "The Comedian" seem almost like a hothouse experiment. As I shall show in the next chapter, Stevens's own voice and tempo are in control of "The Idea of Order" from the first line on. In the first line that control is evident in the firm beats, in its full five beats, the solemnity of the rhythm giving solidity even to the accent on the word "of." "The Comedian," in contrast, is ambiguous, not only in its content—where ambiguity might be a strength—

but also in its style. The querulous questioning toward the end of the poem suggests that the very force driving the poem is turning on itself, self-destructively. It is tempting to say that Stevens himself, and not just his comic mask, is washed away by magnitude, that his will is infected by doubt, by the fear that he in truth is no more than a euphuistic dandy. There is no such doubt in the finest poems of *Harmonium;* but those are the shorter poems. The strenuous, constructive force required of a long poem and so evident beginning with "The Man with the Blue Guitar" is missing in "The Comedian as the Letter C." The poem is brilliant, without a doubt, but the underside of feeling goes soft, becomes spiteful and indulgent by turns; and these are not the feelings being given shape but the feelings of the very act of shaping itself. As a result, they do not complicate and enrich the poem, but rather undermine it.

3

The Poem of the Mind in the Act

I

The great poems between *Harmonium* and *Transport to Summer* are poems of discovery. All of Stevens's genuine poems may be called poems "of the mind in the act of finding / What will suffice." The very movements, however, of the great poems of this period have to do with the act of discovering the significance of the discovery that poems are "of the mind in the act of finding / What will suffice." There are fine poems in *Parts of a World* composed on the basis of this discovery, and there are fine poems in *Harmonium* which reveal the truth of the discovery without an awareness of it; but in the poems to be considered here Stevens is making the crucial discoveries which explain the major changes in his poems from *Harmonium* to *Transport to Summer*. The three poems most clearly central to the changes are "The Idea of Order at Key West," "The Man on the Dump," and "Asides on the Oboe."

"The Idea of Order at Key West" is, without a doubt, the most revolutionary poem written by Stevens. It marks his release from a fictitious notion of poetic concreteness and his realization of the nature of genuine poetic concrescence. In much of *Harmonium* the poet is raging in the chains of ego-centrism. Stevens seems to feel that the poetic voice must speak out of a realized scene, that he as poet must form an image of a person within a scene and then evoke his own sensitive responses as those of the imagined person. Stevens cannot, however, be satisfied with such a predicament; he is dimly aware that he is not the person with whom he has identified himself, that he cannot be that egocenter within a scene, because as poet he has created the scene as well as the ego within it. From this uneasiness comes Yvor Winters's displeasure at Stevens's romantic irony; from this, the uncontrolled violence, the sense of inadequacy in so many of these poems, from the longest, "The Comedian as the Letter C," to a short poem like "The Doctor of Geneva." Winters felt that Stevens's ego-centric predicament was a dead end.[1] Instead, this very failure of so many of these poems is the negative side, the ferment of distress, the premonition of the great poetry to come.

"The Doctor of Geneva" is a most peculiar poem.

> The doctor of Geneva stamped the sand
> That lay impounding the Pacific swell,
> Patted his stove-pipe hat and tugged his shawl.
>
> Lacustrine man had never been assailed
> By such long-rolling opulent cataracts,
> Unless Racine or Bossuet held the like.
>
> He did not quail. A man so used to plumb
> The multifarious heavens felt no awe
> Before these visible, voluble delugings,
>
> Which yet found means to set his simmering mind
> Spinning and hissing with oracular
> Notations of the wild, the ruinous waste,

> Until the steeples of his city clanked and sprang
> In an unburgherly apocalypse.
> The doctor used his handkerchief and sighed.[2]

The poet is at one with the doctor and his contempt for the doctor is violent enough to make the poem seem suicidal. The doctor comes to stand by the Pacific, to endure its violence, to suffer the collapse of all his ordered values under the force of "the ruinous waste," and to experience an apocalyptic vision of vastness within which he and all that he stands for seems pathetically infinitesimal. The tone of the poem, Stevens's own feelings about the experience, is a raw contradiction between contemptuous pity and mocking admiration.

> He did not quail. A man so used to plumb
> The multifarious heavens felt no awe
> Before these visible, voluble delugings

The poet is impressed and yet he clearly recognizes the absurdity of the doctor's bravery. The doctor should have been awestruck. With his traditional, imaginary notions of sublimity, of heavens where a stern but caring Father governed, he was not truly prepared for this waste. And the poet sees himself as like the doctor. He comes to the violence of the Pacific equipped with his Latinic vocabulary, with "Lacustrine" and "opulent cataracts" and "multifarious heavens" and "visible, voluble delugings." How can he survive, with such orderly equipment, the Teutonic violence of "Spinning and hissing" and "clanked and sprang"? In truth, the writing of the poem, the rounding it off in metered rhythm, is an utterly absurd and inadequate response to the vast power, as pathetic and contemptible as the doctor's gesture: "The doctor used his handkerchief and sighed." Such contempt for poetry makes Winters's diagnosis, that Stevens has written poems to the effect that he should write no more, a perception of genius. Yet Stevens, to write such a poem, had to be more vigorous than that. Obviously enough, from our perspective, he and no one else created the Teutonic violence of the poem with his own imagination and set it in opposition to his own and the doctor's lacustrine smallness. Thus, the power to escape, the power of becoming, as a poet, that "ruinous waste" and redeeming it humanly, is implicit in this very poem. The power is there, raging for release, as yet unable to find an outlet. Only later, when aware that the poetry within him is truly like that ruinous waste, could Stevens write of poetry as a destructive force: "The lion sleeps in the sun. / Its nose is on its paws. / It can kill a man."[3] It almost did kill Wallace Stevens. Or, if it did kill him, then "The Idea of Order at Key West" is his resurrection.

"The Idea of Order at Key West" has been inadequately interpreted mainly because it has been treated as too much like Stevens's earlier poems, of which "The Doctor of Geneva" is an example.[4] Too much of the meaning of the poem has been heaped upon the woman who walked by the sea, "the single artificer of the world / In which she sang." Stevens strove to pack all the meaning of "The Doctor of Geneva" into the doctor himself; thus the violence of the poem. In "The Idea of Order at Key West," however, the elemental impulse of the poem, its basic action, the "Blessed rage for order," is identified not only with the woman but also with the questioning of Ramon Fernandez and the poet, with the poet himself as writer of the poem and, through him with "The ever-hooded, tragic-gestured sea," and, finally, through the address to "Pale Ramon" with the reader-critic who, in reading the poem, carries on the spiritual act of the poem, the "Blessed rage for order." "The Idea of Order at Key West" is the first of Stevens's poems which is truly "The poem of the mind in the act," in the precise sense given the phrase in "Of Modern Poetry."[5] The act itself, in the present, the immediate rage for order, is the spirit that dominates the poem, and it belongs to all who participate in it.

Ramon Fernandez, tell me, if you know,
Why, when the singing ended and we turned
Toward the town, tell why the glassy lights,
The lights in the fishing boats at anchor there,
As the night descended, tilting in the air,
Mastered the night and portioned out the sea,
Fixing emblazoned zones and fiery poles,
Arranging, deepening, enchanting night.

Oh! Blessed rage for order, pale Ramon,
The maker's rage to order words of the sea,
Words of the fragrant portals, dimly-starred,
And of ourselves and of our origins,
In ghostlier demarcations, keener sounds.

That Ramon Fernandez is addressed here is particularly appropriate. His book *Messages: Literary Essays,* first published in 1927, is dominated by a sense of spiritual action much like the dominant sense of this poem. In his essay on George Meredith, where he captures this sense most acutely, he says that for Meredith

> sensation, imagination, will, and intelligence are closely bound up and *contemporaneous:* he creates . . . what he understands, in such a way that his creation incessantly modifies reality without betraying it. . . . The known depends greatly on the nature of the act of knowing.[6]

The answer to the question asked of Fernandez, an answer fully present as implication in the poem and only reinforced by Fernandez's ideas, is that the reason one sees the lights master the night is most evidently the "Blessed rage for order," the rage not simply of the woman singing but also, and even more, the rage of the poet Wallace Stevens ordering the woman's ordering of the sea. The singing, the dominant music we have heard throughout the poem, is not that of the woman but of Stevens. He has been ordering her singing throughout

66

the poem, from his superb opening lines, "She sang beyond the genius of the sea" until "the singing ended." Stevens's seeing the lights master the night is not a carry-over and echo from what the woman was doing; it is rather a continuation of what he, as the living, present poet, has been doing all along with the woman's singing. The central ratio is not: as the woman to the sea, so now Stevens to the lights and night. It is: as Stevens was to the woman and sea, so now is Stevens to the lights and night.

Once the poem is read in this way, the "Blessed rage for order" is truly earned; for all through the poem the level upon level of ordering has been present. Thus "The maker's rage to order words of the sea" refers both to the woman and to the poet. Further, both their acts are much like the movement of the sea, "the words of the sea," here thought of not as transformed by the woman's song but as the sea itself, a third raging for order, a tragic gesturing, tragic because always incomplete and indefinable, and always indefinable because the present act of ordering, this moment of ordering, is always, as an act of fixing, beyond anything fixed. The gesturing is always inconclusive of and thus beyond and containing any identifiable gesture. The mind is in the act, within it, encompassed by it, and the act, the dominance in every moment of the act as a rage for order is, by its very nature, the cause, the reason, of one's failure to achieve order.

The last three lines of the poem, which are usually slighted, become transparent and forceful in the light of this reading. The "portals" are any raging words of ordering which lead one on to his own act of ordering; they are fragrant because the stir of beauty itself; they are "dimly-starred" because one is always moved from the fixed to the unfixed, lured by stars but into the dimness, the indefinableness, of one's own immediate, unfixable act of ordering. The words are always of ourselves because in the act of discerning someone's rage for order we find a counterpart of our own very present act; they are of our origins, because the very source of ourselves, our acts of raging, is the "idea" of the act itself. They come "In ghostlier demarcations" because one is distinguishing between a fixed fact that one has raged to order or is raging to order "out there," in the objectified scene, and the unfixable act of making that other act a fact; ghostlier, because it drives one always beyond the materialized fact to the spiritual or ghostly act; and, finally, in keener sounds, because these latest sounds have gained intensity by blending together the sounds of the other, parallel acts within the immediate act that is themselves.

Furthermore, because this conclusion is addressed to that highly articulate critic-reader, Ramon Fernandez, it may be said that this, our rage to order Stevens's rage for order, this poetical-critical act, is identical and opposite to Stevens's own raging; and that the experience of reading the poem, one's effort to grasp it as an immediate experience of feeling and thinking, of listening and speaking, is another level of raging that is, by evident implication, an essential part of the poem.

The title of the poem, it may already be apparent, should be read in such a way as to suggest that the very idea of order at Key West is absurd. From this point on, it will be a most damaging error to think of Stevens's poetry as egocentric. The ego, if we are at all sensitive to the way the word and idea have taken on an objectified, analyzable status in our culture, is fundamentally alien to his new poetry. There will be no more stamping and patting and tugging of human action into the shape of a fixed fact; the movement will be all the other way. Even such an act of boxing-in will be presented in such a way as to accentuate the act, not the box or its contents.

Finally, the rage stirring in one's immediate act is a blessed rage. It is like the sea in being "ever-hooded," for once exposed it is no longer act but fact; and it is "tragic-gestured" like the sea because it is always reaching for what it cannot achieve, an order which, if finally achieved, would destroy the rage that

68

is one's very self. It is, however, unlike the sea because not "fluttering / Its empty sleeves"; its fluttering is full, resonant with all the gesturing and singing which it has heard and rearticulated. "The grinding water and the gasping wind" stirred in the woman's phrase; both stir in the poet's phrases; all three stir in our rearticulation of the poem. Stevens has succeeded, in this poem, in transforming "The lion locked in stone" into "the lion in the lute." He has freed himself from the fictitious notion that poetry must be concrete, an illusion of reality, and has created a concrescent "poem of the mind in the act."

II

"The Man on the Dump" is the second of these major poems of discovery in the middle period of Stevens's career.[7] The poem is based upon the acceptance of a discovery, like that of "The Idea of Order at Key West," that everything is unreal, is trash, as fact, and that reality is the very insecurity of "the mind in the act," in the present act. In this poem, however, Stevens goes beyond his previous sense of the world; what should be the climax of the poem, on the basis of that earlier discovery, proves empty, and, out of this crisis, Stevens moves to a deeper and surer sense of the chaos of the poetic world of which he writes, and writing makes. The climax that fails and thus provokes a crisis is the fourth of the five stanzas of the poem:

> That's the moment when the moon creeps up
> To the bubbling of bassoons. That's the time
> One looks at the elephant-colorings of tires.
> Everything is shed; and the moon comes up as the moon
> (All its images are in the dump) and you see
> As a man (not like an image of a man),
> You see the moon rise in the empty sky.

Surely all readers have been at least slightly disturbed by this stanza. In the first two stanzas, Stevens has been developing his sense of the emptiness of most images, the triteness even of our images of novelty. He succeeds in making even "dew" seem most stale. Dew and flowers, even these one grows to hate except on the dump. Only as rejected can one tolerate such imagery. In the third stanza, he attacks spring itself with all its flowers, leaving only the smallest point for escape. It is in the present moment, between the past, the rejected flowers, and the future, the flowers to be rejected, that "One feels the purifying change." By the end of this stanza Stevens has put himself in a most difficult situation. Up to this point he has carried on a process of rejection and now we expect the hoard of these destructions, the vital, pure image that survives this destructive act. And Stevens seems to try to give us just this image: "That's the moment when the moon creeps up / To the bubbling of bassoons." Furthermore, Stevens asserts that at this moment things are really as they are, that there is no pretense that what is trash is other than trash. The moon comes up as the moon (not as one of its images, like "the moon Blanche" of the first stanza) and one sees, not as an image of a man, but as a man. "You see the moon rise in the empty sky." One asks, however: Is this the awaited image, and does one feel the purifying change?

It is obviously not the awaited image, although Stevens seems to be presenting it as if it is. At this point the crucial question is: Is there a contradiction between intention and realization? Does the meaning of the stanza, the pure experience of seeing things as they really are, right now, with no metaphorical screens, conflict with one's poetic sense that Stevens simply could not triumph over the dump, one's sense that these "fresh" images are as trite as all the other rejected trash? Then must one say that Stevens's meaning is clear but that the poem fails as a poem? Such an interpretation and characterization lead to such an evaluation.

70

Another reading of the stanza, however, saves the poem and explains its last stanza, which is usually slighted, except for the last line. A part of the realized sense of the fourth stanza is that it too is trash. Why else would Stevens use "creeps up" in the first line? The phrase recalls the first lines of the poem:

> Day creeps down. The moon is creeping up.
> The sun is a corbeil of flowers the moon Blanche
> Places there, a bouquet. Ho-ho . . .

Those lines express a dumpish attitude. The poet is being novel, calling the moon Blanche and having her place the sun on the horizon as a bouquet. How clever! How dull! Likewise, one must say that "the bubbling of bassoons" is clever and dull, as is "the elephant-colorings of tires." Stevens is trying here too to be novel. One feels the strain, but also the sense of failure, the mere oddity and arbitrariness of the imagery.

Our disappointment in the stanza, in other words, is part of the realized poem; the stanza is poetically meant to be disappointing. The next lines confirm such a reading:

> One sits and beats an old tin can, lard pail.
> One beats and beats for that which one believes.

At this point of crisis the poet has split in two, into the man on the dump who sits there beating and beating the pail, now turned into an image which one can see, and the poet who has withdrawn from the scene and looks at it from a distance. What does he see? He sees the man on the dump being repetitious, being the very opposite of fresh and changing and novel. And he realizes that the repetition and boredom of the first three stanzas did not lie in the images used, in the "freshness of night" and the "freshness of morning," in the dew and the flowers, but in the way the man on the dump was using the images. He was generalizing rather than individualizing them; and anything becomes repetitious if one thinks of it as gen-

71

eral, as unchanging in its various instances. In his present mood the man on the dump could not but be bored with anything that occurred. He imagines even a new image like "You see the moon rise in the empty sky" with a sense that it is about to be trash. His mood is ennui, he is dominated by the belief that all is trash, that "Days pass like papers from a press." It is just in such a state, in such boredom, that the split of these lines can occur, that one can become detached from his immediate ego and look down at it as it really is.

From this perspective one sees that an image is fresh or boring, novel or trite according to the way one receives it. The quality of the crow's voice is inferior to, depends upon, the ear that hears it; the nightingale is not commonplace if the ear and heart and mind that respond to it are pained deeply by it; peevish birds may provide solace, depending on the ear that hears them. The blatter of grackles may indeed, if transformed by this person and not that, come out as Invisible priest. The truth then is that nothing, except this very truth, is true absolutely: every truth is the truth, but only for the ear and heart and mind taking it in and believing it. The truth is that vital human experience is made up of endless truths, each of which is "the truth" for the person believing it, but each of which is "a truth" from the detached perspective of the man on the dump become poet. Even this, of course, is but a truth. It is the truth for the poet of this poem. There is no "the truth" except the truth that every truth is but "a truth." "A truth" is not even "a truth," however, unless it is "the truth" to the person experiencing it. Thus, this poem of boredom is, in its effect, the very opposite. It affirms, gaily and expansively, out of its very boredom, the value, the freshness, the novelty of the trashiest, of the tritest images, according to the person responding to and believing them. It affirms the beauty of the ugliest things, of "mattresses of the dead, / Bottles, pots, shoes" if they are received by one in such a mood that he murmurs "aptest eve."

In sum, the thing known, as Fernandez said of Meredith, depends on the act of knowing, the image believed on the act of believing. The truth is that in "The poem of the mind in the act" Stevens must now recognize that the very present act is vital and real, is the way things really are, only according to the mood, the heart, the mind, of the person acting it out. The very boredom of this poem arises naturally from a discovery as exhilarating as that of "The Idea of Order at Key West." If only the living present is of value, then yesterday and all that it contains become of no value except as yesterday, except as trash rejected from the present. The next, frightening step is the feeling that even the things of the present cannot be believed in with much conviction since one knows they are about to become trash. It is out of this impossible predicament, another opportunity for poetic suicide, that Stevens makes the second of his major discoveries of this transitional period, the discovering of the marvelous value of there being "so many selves," each with its own "sensuous world."[8] The affirmation is not, to be sure, contained within any single lines in "The Man on the Dump." Moments of climax disappoint, and one moves from line to line, thoroughly discontented. The burst of awareness and vitality comes straight out of, and circles beyond, the last line of the poem: "Where was it one first heard of the truth? The the." "The the." All the meaning of the poem explodes out of those two words: the truth is there is no "the truth," that every "the truth" is "a truth"; but, conversely, the truth is that every "a truth," even to be "a truth," must be "the truth," the real, sensuous world, of the self believing it.

A sullen pedant might retort that such a reading illustrates the fallacy of imitative form, turning a poor poem into a great one by an overreading of its weakest lines. A retort like this is respectable because it confirms a central truth about the reading and criticism of poetry: that meaning and significance, that interpretation and judgment, that characterization and evaluation are absolutely inseparable. One values the poem so much because he understands it the way he does; he understands it the way he does because he values it so much. The circularity of fact and value, of philology and criticism, is the central truth to be insisted upon for the serious reading of poetry. Such a position is not so tolerant as Stevens's "The Man on the Dump" would prefer, although one can admit that the error of those who separate interpretation and criticism has instrumental value. That is, it provides the opposition which allows for a precise statement of truth; for all affirmation is negation.

Parts of a World contains a number of poems which are written out of the liberating sense achieved through the struggle and distress of "The Man on the Dump," and several of these are actually more organically whole than this poem. One of the curious things about "The Man on the Dump" is its lack of organic wholeness, at least in the ordinary meaning of that phrase. It would, I think, be impossible to predict, on the basis of the first three lines of the poem, that the poem would go where it does in the fifth stanza. Reading the poem properly, even if for the hundredth time, one must and does read the fourth stanza expecting it to work, expecting it to provide "the purifying change." That it does not entails a breakdown. As a result, one tends to read the fifth stanza rather hurriedly, not expecting the lines to mean much, until he comes to the last line, which he easily gives meaning to because he has also read the little poem which follows, "On the Road Home," a simple poem which takes away one's sense of the opaqueness of "The Man on the Dump," the sense that its objects are in excess of its meaning. One has been trained to treat poems as artifacts, not as action and struggle, not as the concrescence of a whole human act, working itself out with feeling, passion, imagination, will, and intellect. Thus, even after discovering how this poem builds poetically on a major poetic error, a reader may prefer Stevens's securer and less disruptive poems. If he does, however, he will be violating one of the crucial aspects of Stevens's sense of "The poem of the mind in the act."

"Connoisseur of Chaos" and "Landscape with Boat" are two poems which develop an experience much like that of "The Man on the Dump," but with more assurance and quite evidently without the sense of vital discovery that makes the Dump poem so extraordinary. "Study of Two Pears" is a superbly assured exercise illustrating the triumphant discovery of "The Man on the Dump."[9] Its first, fifth, and last stanzas are as follows:

I
Opusculum paedogogum.
The pears are not viols,
Nudes or bottles.
They resemble nothing else.

V
The yellow glistens.
It glistens with various yellows,
Citrons, oranges and greens
Flowering over the skin.

VI
The shadows of the pears
Are blobs on the green cloth.
The pears are not seen
As the observer wills.

Stevens is wonderfully funny with his pedagogue. Every line affirms the will of the teacher, his determination, his insistence, that these pears are as they are. He obviously loves the pears, sensuously, as "Citrons, oranges and greens / Flowering over the skin" manifests. "The pears are not seen / As the observer wills" because the pedagogue carrying out this demonstration wills that they are not to be seen as the observer wills. In other words, such hard-headed, objective realism is

75

a most willful affair. But Stevens is only partly making fun of his speaker. "A truth" must be "the truth" of him who affirms it, or else it is not even a truth. And, to be sure, as many critics have pointed out, in some poems Stevens himself accepts the pedagogue's truth as the truth.[10] In this poem, however, he most certainly does not. His high spirits, the hilarity of the poem, depend upon the contradictory willfulness with which the realist insists that the will is not involved in the way the pears are seen. The poem is neat, a perfectly shaped artifact, though of course its shape is all in the feelings, the inner, only implicit sense which poet and reader share, beyond the sensibleness of the pedagogue. Such assurance depends on the achieved sense the struggle for which is realized in "The Man on the Dump." Nothing is so comforting as to be this sure of the limits of so assured a man as the pedagogue is.

III

Of all Stevens's great poems, the third major one of this period of transition, "Asides on the Oboe," is most in need of critical performance.[11] The interpreters have attended to it. We know there are two kinds of oboe or hautboy: the one of the sixteenth century used for fanfares to introduce the king after the prologues are over; and the one we know as ours, popular from the early eighteenth century on, a plaintive, solitary, delicate, questioning instrument. We know the referent of "the wide river in / An empty land," and who Boucher was and the nature of his art. Indeed, we could all no doubt provide a scholarly paraphrase of the poem. But this is like memorizing the notes of a Handel sonata in preparation for making it into music; it is like a dress rehearsal in an empty theater done by sleepwalkers, quite empty and dead, a simple polishing of the shell. It is necessary to know the meanings of the words of a poem, and knowing them means, for the scholarly interpreter, knowing their meanings as used in the immediate cultural ambience of the poem, in other poems and in speeches and letters of the poet in question, and in the works of his contemporaries. These meanings, however, are, at best, preparatory; they are not the meanings of the words in the poem, meanings which become unique when charged with the significance of this single poem as an action, as elemental feeling breaking into diamonds in the light of the sun. They undergo a profound sea-change, eyes become pearls; what seemed discrete is caught up and suffused by the poet's basic sense of his world. On the other hand, a performance like that provided several years ago by John Ciardi is not adequate either.[12] Ciardi most effectively makes the poem baffling, stirring up the sense that knowing the meanings of the words in the poem is truly next to nothing, and mainly distracts one from the profoundly moving quality of the poem. One desires not obscurity but elucidation, but elucidation which sweeps a light across the swelling torrent, not one which blacks the torrent out and pretends it does not exist.

"Asides on the Oboe" affirms a final belief in the tragedian not the tragic hero, the poet instead of his creatures, Sophocles not Oedipus, Shakespeare not Lear, Homer and not Achilles. It is not a belief in an individual tragedian, but in the fiction of the tragedian. It is just as emphatically not a belief in a philosophical idea or concept of the poet. It is, instead, one of the Vichian *generi fantastici, gli universali o caratteri poetici,* "imaginative types, poetic universals or characters." It is like Achilles, an identification of an individual hero and the hero; it is like MacCullough who is also the MacCullough; it is like a truth which is the truth. It is a fiction and it is the fiction of the maker of fictions. What sets this fiction off from all others is that it accepts things as they are; it does not bowdlerize or falsify. All the passions of the sea of being are received and transformed poetically, the wine-dark sea into milky lines, bestial violence into immaculate imagery.

The fiction one believes in is not an individual man, not

oneself or any other man, even as poet. Stevens is not, whatever has been said to the contrary, an Adamic poet. The situation of the poem is most closely analogous to that of Dante in the twenty-sixth canto of *Paradiso*. He is in the eighth heaven of the fixed stars and has just been introduced by Beatrice to Adam. Dante supplicates Adam to speak to him, says he knows Adam understands his wish, even to knowing the unspoken questions he wishes answered. Adam replies:

> Sanz' essermi proferta
> da te, la voglia tua discerno meglio
> che tu qualunque cosa t' è più certa;
> perch' io la veggio nel verace speglio
> che fa di sè pareglio all'altre cose,
> e nulla face lui di sè pareglio.[13]

Adam discerns Dante's wish, his need, better than Dante ever could understand anything about himself, because he sees it as reflected through God, because he sees it in the veracious mirror which makes itself the like of every other thing but makes nothing like onto it. In "Asides on the Oboe," as in all Stevens's later poems, an inner, intimate community is evoked and each speaker is transparent to the other, as Dante here to Adam; all is transparent because all is under the sign of, all is being made and seen and imagined by, that veracious mirror, that "globe, responsive / As a mirror with a voice." The speaking voice is Adam's, but Adam is in Paradise, he is seeing experience in the perfect mirror, in the supreme fiction, in God not as he is but as he might be, as the central man, the human globe. Stevens in the poem then is not merely Stevens, he is also the Stevens, this imaginative realization of the imagination. Furthermore, whereas he speaks, as Paradisal Adam, with the authority of a Shakespearian hautboy, affirming his faith, he is also the questioner, the mortal man, unsure and skeptical, Dante the suppliant, *come il baccellier*, "the student," who speaks with the voice of Handel's hautboy, saying that "man is not enough, / Can never stand as god, is ever wrong / In the end, however naked, tall." Indeed, the true force of the poem stems from the anguish of Dante's need, from the plaintive, suffering oboe. Surely one does not make his asides with the same instrument on which he puffs forth his fanfare. It is out of doubt and pain, out of their resistance, that the poem grows, expands, and in the end finds what will suffice, a harmonious oneness of both oboes, of Dante and Adam, of Stevens the doubter and Stevens the affirmer, within the poetic fiction, the glass man, all inner, because, as the last line affirms, "without external reference."

In the earlier of his two essays on Stevens, Randall Jarrell had asked why no one had ever given Stevens a copy of R. G. Collingwood's *The Principles of Art,* where it is argued that art is never merely a craft.[14] But the poet who wrote "Asides on the Oboe" had read Collingwood, or had thought out at least one of Collingwood's key ideas by himself, the idea that genuine art is a perpetual battle against the corruption of consciousness.[15] The poet, according to Collingwood, in writing a poem, is exploring his feelings and consciously articulating them. The very poem is the exploration, the shaping, of the feelings which he apprehends imaginatively. Now he may dislike the shape he is giving to what he has apprehended; it may be troublesome and may contradict his sense of himself. He may wish so much to believe something that he must exclude the feelings of doubt which he apprehends within himself. As a result, he excludes the troublesome aspects of his feeling from his poem. What he includes is true, but the exclusions bowdlerize the poem, they make it an instance of what Collingwood calls the corrupt consciousness. Poetic immaculateness is inclusion of all that is felt within the exploratory shaping of the poem; corruption is exclusive of what offends. This notion of innocence, incidentally, is the basis of the poem which follows "Asides" in Stevens's *Collected Poems.* At the beginning of "Extracts from Addresses to the Academy of Fine Ideas," Stevens rejects with sorrow the simpler notion of the innocent eye, the idea that one can see a thing so truly that it is unaffected by one's own act of seeing it. From this rejection he moves to a notion of innocence that is Socratic, that takes in all, that evades or hides from nothing. This innocence is the virtue of the supreme fiction, and its presence makes "Asides on the Oboe" the dramatic, disrupted, and finally earned harmony that it is.

The drama is implicit in the first three lines:

> The prologues are over. It is a question, now,
> Of final belief. So, say that final belief
> Must be in a fiction. It is time to choose.

The affirmer has had enough preliminary fuss. He puts a sharp period to the "The prologues are over." He cannot, however, escape the doubter for a moment. The doubter, of course, is the one who has been emphasizing the fictive nature of one's beliefs all along. The affirmer must concede his reason, even if bitingly and painfully: thus the accent ending the second line forces a pause and heavy accent on the first word of the third line, "Must," and this heaviness in turn forces one to whip rapidly over the next three words, then hitting the fifth syllable, "fiction," with as much heaviness as was on the "Must." He grants all. He has to. But with gritted teeth he insists "It is time to choose," with three stiff accents and some force even on the two unaccented syllables.

Then he begins his first affirmative sweep with the uncontested rejection of three heroic fictions thought by some to be alternatives to the poetic fiction, even in our time. The religious fiction that the waste land can miraculously become a garden is obsolete. It differs from the poetic fiction because, unlike it, it pretends that by miracle bloody martyrdoms become jasmine islands, that pain is pleasure, death life, blood beauty. The pastoral gods, idyllically languid and content, so decadently fat and immobile in Boucher's art, are soiled images of peace in a world without war, as if there could be good without evil, a good in abstract stasis that kills itself by its very purity. Military heroes are rejected because "time granulates" them; that is, they accept bloody martyrdoms as good in themselves, man as a granule, as an item, as non-inclusive, as locked in isolation, beast against beast, as a value in itself which it is not. Stevens's fiction, the impossible possible man of Aristotle's, that is, the poet, must be innocent in the inclusive sense: he must recognize that jasmine islands become bloody martyrdoms, but he must not see human life as merely bloody; yet he is not permitted to bring off the inclusion in human life of both evil and good, of good even in the midst of war, by means of a miracle. By asking so much of his poetic fiction, Stevens is making things as hard as possible for himself. He must, of course, since he is not only affirmer but doubter; he is willing to make these difficult assertions, even so, because in his faith he feels he writes under the influence of the poetic, fictive force. Tonally, this first stanza is the most undisrupted hymn of praise in the entire poem, with the "om"-like repetitions of sound and alliteration of

> Still by the sea-side mutters milky lines
> Concerning an immaculate imagery.

and the extraordinary assonance and consonance of the last three words of the stanza:

> Who in a million diamonds sums us up.

Although the second stanza might seem more unqualifiedly affirmative than the first, and though in mere content it may be so, its tone undermines it. Out of the triumphant hymn of the first stanza comes the cockiness and the preciosity, the arrogance of the aesthete, of the second stanza. Stevens lets

81

the aesthete have his say, but mocks him by the tone. What is said in this stanza, in effect, is that the world is composed by the poetic imagination; the fragments of the world become parts of a whole only through the force of man's imagination. The year indeed is divided into twelve months, so that August is August, only because men have imagined it so. And, as Denis de Rougemont has argued, the very value and nature of love in the western world, based as it is on the clandestine, dark, adulterous aspects of chivalric love, is a creation of our poets.

There is some truth, to be sure, in these claims, but there is also too much artifice, too much contempt and indifference for nature, for the beast in man, for the impulsive forces of the wine-dark sea. This implicit criticism is in the first two lines, in the unnaturalness of their rhythm:

> He is the transparence of the place in which
> He is and in his poems we find peace.

How dainty a rhythm! One is forced to hit with emphasis "is," "of," "which," "is," "in," and "we." Syntax and meter together force this artifice, this preciousness upon one, especially as the magnificent sweep of the last part of the first stanza still echoes in our ears. Enunciation is a bit too precise to be real. This precious fellow is made of glass, is cold and numbered. If he "dewily cries, / Thou art not August unless I make thee so," surely he does it while adjusting his silk cravat and with a rouged lisp. To be sure, the poetic fiction endures through history and the archaisms of language and syntax are indicative of that. But one does not deny the truth of what is being said in the poem. Adam does see life in the veracious mirror of God; but in this stanza, he has forgotten the fleshly, mortal, doubter Dante; he has committed the sin of arrogance. One hears the cockiness of the voice in every line and laughs at his pretentiousness. Stevens means it so.

As the third stanza manifests!

> One year, death and war prevented the jasmine scent
> And the jasmine islands were bloody martyrdoms.
> How was it then with the central man? Did we
> Find peace?

The naturalness of the first three sentences of this stanza, the fact that the second and third sentences are questions, asked bitterly, in passion and anger, accentuates the falseness of the voice of the second stanza. Even so, this new fleshly voice is part of the supra-temporal poetic fiction, as its use of an obsolete meaning of "prevented," the meaning of "came before" in addition to "kept from happening" indicates. At this point in the poem, one feels that the glass man is transcendental and self-enclosed, perfect and peaceful himself, but excluding from him all men at war, who are abandoned in their pain, desolate in the waste land. Stevens the affirmer, with his back against the wall, declares his credo triumphantly and compellingly. He does here what Raymond Williams claims all modern tragedy tries to do: he comes to terms with death, with bloody martyrdoms, without lying.

The question is, how does he do it, why do we feel that these concluding lines

> It was not as if the jasmine ever returned.
> But we and the diamond globe at last were one.
> We had always been partly one. It was as we came
> To see him, that we were wholly one, as we heard
> Him chanting for those buried in their blood,
> In the jasmine haunted forests, that we knew
> The glass man, without external reference.

are an achieved harmony, that the oneness of Dante and Adam in God, of Stevens and the Stevens in the philosophers' man, of suffering man and poet in Poetry, are an experienced rather than a merely asserted harmony? How can this be? How can we accept the stark fact that a man we love dies and is buried in his blood without redemption, without any hope of a life

83

after death? How can we keep from being brutalized, from accepting the metal heroes that time granulates as the only kind of man there is, man killing man, ephemeral, with no value beyond his brutality? Stevens will not allow, in this fictive but not fictitious world, for any blinking at the facts or for any pious hopes. All that poetic fiction provides beyond ourselves—and yet it is all we need, is indeed what we most need—is a chant "for those buried in their blood, / In the jasmine haunted forests." It is that poetically we recall the love and beauty which has been irretrievably lost; it is this haunting memory that gives to the sacrifice of those who die in pain such value; it is the memory of love that makes its loss so grievous; it is the grief, the suffering, that sustains our sense of the value of what is lost. Without the memory of beauty, death and blood and pain would cease to be loss, would cease to be martyrdom, and we would all become unfeeling beasts, along with the metal heroes. In truth, that would be a pleasanter condition than the one we share with Stevens and his poetic fiction. Since Stevens is no hedonist, however, this should be no surprise. He is a humanist, a poetic humanist, whose ideal is a fiction of innocence and for whom innocence is compassionate awareness, an inclusiveness which accepts evil and pain unblinkingly, and with it the despair and grief and suffering that make man so different from man brutalized. Of all Stevens's poems, "Asides on the Oboe" is his most beautiful tragedy. It is the song of the nightingale, with all its torture in the ear. It is the blatter of grackles hymned forth as Invisible priest, with the day pulled to pieces, the cry of Stanza my stone. It echoes and echoes and echoes in the ear and mind and heart of Ramon Fernandez as he turns from it and looks out upon the world of days that "pass like papers from a press" and transforms it into a world of tragic beauty. It is the world of things as they are, of men like mechanical beetles never quite warm, but played upon the blue guitar, in the blueness of the historical imagination.

84

4

"The Man with the Blue Guitar"

If one begins with the achievement of "The Man with the Blue Guitar," he can trace certain lines backward into conditions that made possible, though not necessary, this, Stevens's first great long poem. Between "The Comedian as the Letter C" and "The Man with the Blue Guitar" Stevens seems to have acquired a strength of will and ease of mind that are not at all apparent in his early work. By 1934 he had become a vice-president of the Hartford Accident and Indemnity Company, and he had purchased his own home of which he says in a letter to James A. Powers, December 19, 1935: "For my part, I never really lived until I had a home, and my own room, say, with a package of books from Paris or London."[1] Confidence and aspiration, a commitment to *la speranza dell' altezza,* "to the hope for excellence," are affirmed, almost as a manifesto in the poem of *Ideas of Order* which Stevens liked best, "How to Live. What to Do."

> There was
> Only the great height of the rock
> And the two of them standing still to rest.
>
> There was the cold wind and the sound
> It made, away from the muck of the land
> That they had left, heroic sound
> Joyous and jubilant and sure.[2]

There is a new ease which permits the daring, a rock that allows Stevens to give himself to the wind.

The new forcefulness and serenity, which underlie the poems discussed in the previous chapter, are also evident in Stevens's first lengthy poem after "The Comedian," "Like Decorations in a Nigger Cemetery." The world of "Decorations" is cluttered and incoherent, but throughout it one feels the presence of a firm will controlling the subtly varied rhythms, which are in marked contrast to the monotonous, flowing opulence of "The Comedian." Each of the short sections of "Decorations" is another beginning, a new assertion of will, which ends inconclusively, suggesting more than it says, often not even achieving the syntactical completeness of a sentence. The end of each section demands a further assertion, and, in fact, "Decorations" as a whole has a strenuous arc of development, the lack of which accounts for much of the flabbiness of "The Comedian." At the beginning, the poet of "Decorations," the sun of autumn, which is passing like Walt Whitman, accepts the eccentric as the base of design and disdains the deadliness of a life of permanence, a life free of death, a life in which death is "a parish death," after which one goes on living the same as before, in heaven or wherever. The poet would have one live a dying life, in which the past dies into the present and the present into the future, not a life with a center, organized according to unvarying rules, established by the rabbis, "Under the mat of frost and over the mat of clouds." But between this initial belief and the conclusion of the poem:

> Union of the weakest develops strength
> Not wisdom. Can all men, together, avenge
> One of the leaves that have fallen in autumn?
> But the wise man avenges by building his city in snow.[8]

Stevens deepens his sense of what it means to live a dying life in the contemporary world. There is, one grants, a certain sameness in the style of the poem from start to finish, in the fact that each section is a new birth which concludes as a dying into silence, so that the next section comes as another beginning, not the necessary consequence of what went before it. At the same time, there is a deeper movement to the poem, which is Stevens's discovery that to live the dying life of the present the poet must accept the mechanical life of the masses, the life that by excluding death is a deeper death than the life that is a constant dying. From a contempt for a life that is fixed "In the muscular poses of the museums" (XVIII) Stevens moves to a partial acceptance of life as "the standard repertoire in line," and thus he asserts:

XLI

The chrysanthemums' astringent fragrance comes
Each year to disguise the clanking mechanism
Of machine within machine within machine.

XLII

God of the sausage-makers, sacred guild,
Or possibly, the merest patron saint
Ennobled as in a mirror to sanctity.

XLIII

It is curious that the density of life
On a given plane is ascertainable
By dividing the number of legs one sees by two.
At least the number of people may thus be fixed.[4]

The unbearable banality of such a life must be borne by the sun as poet, even though he remains aware that such a conception of life is a denial of the nature both of the actual and of poetry:

XXXI
A teeming millpond or a furious mind.
Gray grasses rolling windily away
And bristling thorn-trees spinning on the bank.
The actual is a deft beneficence.

XXXII
Poetry is a finikin thing of air
That lives uncertainly and not for long
Yet radiantly beyond much lustier blurs.[5]

After his sense of tragedy has been enhanced, after "heavy nights of drenching weather," the poet as sun returns compassionately to his people. He knows that the "Union of the weakest" cannot "avenge / One of the leaves that have fallen in autumn," and he insists on building his own city wisely, in snow; but nonetheless he no longer remains aloof from his people, in fastidious contempt. Thus, from an initial rejection of life which excludes poetry by excluding death (which is the mother of beauty), he moves to an acceptance of that deadly life as part of the dying life of poetry.

During the early thirties, with his newly acquired strength, Stevens was trying to move as close as possible to the normal, to the lives of ordinary people. He admits to a commitment to this a few years later in a letter to Hi Simons:

> I began to feel that I was on the edge: that I wanted to get to the center: that I was isolated, and that I wanted to share the common life. . . . People say that I live in a world of my own: that sort of thing. Instead of seeking for a "relentless contact", I have been interested in what might be described as an attempt to achieve the

> normal, the central. . . . Of course, I don't agree with
> the people who say that I live in a world of my own; I
> think that I am perfectly normal, but I see that there is
> a center. For instance, a photograph of a lot of fat men
> and women in the woods, drinking beer and singing
> Hi-li Hi-lo convinces me that there is a normal that I
> ought to try to achieve.[6]

His first effort "to achieve the normal" in a very long poem,
"Owl's Clover," is a regressive failure. In effect, what he does
in this poem is to abandon his exceptional wisdom and pro-
claim the strength of the "Union of the weakest." He tries
to write a poem in which he as poet is "the conformer who
conforms," in which he excludes everything personal and distinctive and becomes one with the masses, giving shape to the
masses. He would carve a statue under this title: *The Mass /
Appoints These Marbles Of Itself To Be / Itself.*[7] To accomplish his purpose, he gives himself up to a style much like
that of "The Comedian." The lines roll unimpededly with
parallel form after parallel form and apposition after apposition; but there is no sealike substance, as there is in "The
Comedian," to give significance to this style. Most of the
images of people are of swarms, of groups of mesdames singing in phantasmal choruses. The God of this world is an utterly objective, transcendental force called Ananke. The de-
sired life is a life in which the thoughts of all are the same
thought. The ideal is to be pure being, devoid of becoming, a
life lived

> For the gaudium of being, Jocundus instead
> Of the black-blooded scholar, the man of the cloud, to be
> The medium man among other medium men,
> The cloak to be clipped, the night to be re-designed,
> Its land-breath to be stifled, its color changed,
> Night and the imagination being one.[8]

The art needed for this new life is to be the very opposite of the art of "The Idea of Order at Key West." It is to be objective, an object, a massive statue, immovable, supreme, untouched by the shaping hand of the poet.

"Owl's Clover" is a self-destructive poem. Instead of trying to incorporate the montonous, anonymous strength of the masses into his own aspiring wisdom, Stevens capitulates completely, throwing his whole self, with all its acquired intricacies, into a massive stasis in which the value of human life is ascertained "By dividing the number of legs one sees by two." It was a desperate enterprise from which Stevens must at some time have recoiled in horror. It was the one major betrayal of his poetic genius. Having let the monster go into print, he could do nothing but revise it futilely and then resolutely exclude the whole thing from the *Collected Poems*. And of course redeem himself by writing "The Man with the Blue Guitar."

In "The Man with the Blue Guitar" Stevens fuses his *speranza dell' altezza*, "his need and hope for sublime excellence," with his need "to share the common life"; and he does so in such a way as to achieve his first great long poem. The elemental act of "The Blue Guitar" is the reconciling of the exceptional man as poet and the ordinariness of common men; and the reconciliation is worked out as the poet comes to realize that he contains ordinariness within himself even while remaining the exceptional poet he is. The poem is an original synthesis of the major forces with which Stevens was pressing outward against the violent and chaotic pressures of his time. The tremendous constructive force of the poet, evident in the dry, decisive lines of the poem, fuses with his openness to the needs of his people. Neither the ordinary nor the extraordinary is sacrificed or compromised. It could almost be said that by this poem alone Stevens has given a durable and endurable shape to the quality of the life of his country.

Undoubtedly, "The Man with the Blue Guitar" is one of the most difficult of Stevens's poems to explicate. Even so, no other of his long poems is more evidently unified in its content, style, tone, and mood. It holds together poetically, and thus one cannot rest easy in the fragmentariness of his own analytical comments about it. He must go beyond an interpretation that accepts the poem as merely the "incessant conjunctioning of things as they are and things imagined";[9] that refers to the thirty-three parts of the poem as "independent but thematically interrelated lyrics"; that finds that "in no other poem will the unity of the work be so tenuous"; and that claims that Stevens "imposes an aesthetic cosmos upon physical chaos."[10] Even the following statement by Stevens concerning the parts of the poem, "I kept them in their original order for my own purposes, because one really leads into another, even when the relationship is only one of contrast," does not do justice to the powerful dramatic unity of "The Blue Guitar."[11]

There are, to be sure, obvious reasons for this poem's remaining impervious to criticism. Without a narrative sequence, it lacks even a skeletal framework like the three parts of the "Notes toward a Supreme Fiction" which have so often misled critics into taking the frame as an adequate substitute for the underlying, unifying, ordering pulsion of feeling that makes that poem as great an achievement as "The Blue Guitar" is. Furthermore, recurrent imagery—and there is no doubt more of it in this poem than in the "Notes"—does not provide the ready handle sought by the non-poetic reader. Blue, green, the sun, the moon, the sea, earth and space, the guitar and lute and various songs, the flies, beetles, lion, monster, giant, the hero of bearded bronze and the pagan in a varnished car, the air and the turgid sky and the overcast weather, these images and their variations change in meaning and feeling almost as often as they are used. There are indeed no ready handles; only if one attends with the eye of a hawk to the underlying action of the poem, to the mind in the act of finding what will suffice, can he experience and understand

and then, if fortunate, articulate the forceful and profoundly significant unity of the poem.

There is a crucial and most difficult distinction that must be made and kept continually in mind in the reading of these later poems of Stevens concerning poetry and the poet. It is the distinction between the poet and poetry as defined and imagined within the poem and the very poem itself in which the poet is shaping and defining and imagining poetry and the poet in their relations to those things which, to some extent, differ from them. If this distinction is blurred or ignored, or if the present, shaping act of the poet into a poem is reduced to the poet as shaped, then one's criticism is reduced to a criticism of content alone and the individual form of the poem is sacrificed to the theories which it contains and which may be considered independently of the form without apparent loss. The neglect of this distinction lies behind much recent criticism of Stevens and explains why it often sounds like old-fashioned philology instead of genuine criticism. The talk is of poetry and the poet, but its manner is to reduce poetry and the poet to content which does not truly differ from poetic material, to ideas and images which are the same in the poem as they would be outside the poem, as if the form of the poem made no difference to their nature. Such confusion is utterly destructive of the best of Stevens's poems during this period because their genuine forms are acts of struggle, are actions which overcome fixities and oppositions in order to achieve a climactic reconciliation of all resistances. At the climax, and only then, the poet as present, acting shaper and the poet as the fact shaped become one, and the movement of struggle is stilled in momentary finality. In "The Man with the Blue Guitar," several sections are pauses in which an opposition has been overcome; but then, out of the tranquil pause a new doubt or problem arises which requires that the poet press onward to a higher resolution. As I said in an earlier essay, it is only in the thirtieth section of the poem that Stevens achieves the finest reconciliation of which he is capable in this poem.[12] Even after this achievement, however, three more sections follow in which Stevens qualifies and clarifies his achieved stance.

In the thirtieth section Stevens does what he could not do at the beginning: he evolves a man, in his essential nature.

> From this I shall evolve a man.
> This is his essence: the old fantoche
>
> Hanging his shawl upon the wind,
> Like something on the stage, puffed out,
>
> His strutting studied through centuries.
> At last, in spite of his manner, his eye
>
> A-cock at the cross-piece on a pole
> Supporting heavy cables, slung
>
> Through Oxidia, banal suburb,
> One-half of all its installments paid.
>
> Dew-dapper clapper-traps, blazing
> From crusty stacks above machines.
>
> Ecce, Oxidia is the seed
> Dropped out of this amber-ember pod,
>
> Oxidia is the soot of fire,
> Oxidia is Olympia.

What he evolves, as a result of all the struggle that has preceded this section, is a man as poet, an ordinary man who sees with exceptional poetic insight. Stevens evolves this poet-man historically, and his history is the very story of the whole of "The Man with the Blue Guitar." At first the poet as conceived by the poet is an "old fantoche" with most pretentious ideas about himself. He is merely a puppet who puffs himself up by "Hanging his shawl upon the wind." He is like "a hero's head, large eye / And bearded bronze, but not a man." At this point, the poet is merely exceptional; he has not recognized his ordinariness; he thinks of himself not as "the lion in the lute," a monster clawing on the blue guitar, but as a hero magnified, at one with the weather of his stage, a vast shadow hunched over a guitar which is at one with "the overcast blue / Of the air." Only in the end, in spite of "His strutting studied through centuries," does he come to look at things as they really are; and then he comes to see that his true environment is "Oxidia, banal suburb, / One-half of all its installments paid." Nonetheless, this man-poet, recognizing his ordinariness, views it with all his history in his bones. He looks at "a pole / Supporting heavy cables, slung / Through Oxidia," with a sense that this pole and its cross-piece have replaced the Cross, that his present clear sight is a passion, a suffering, with a sense that he has died to his man-godliness and has become a mere man. As man-poet, then, as one who sees Oxidia only in the light of Olympia, who sees the forest as "jasmine-haunted," he is exceptional; he is a mere man, but he is in the lute. He observes the sooty suburb, Oxidia, but speaks out his seeing with terms snatched from the fire of Olympia:

> Dew-dapper clapper-traps, blazing
> From crusty stacks above machines.

Are these words spoken by Stevens the poet shaping this poem? Yes, but they are also spoken by the man-poet to whom he has given shape. Here at last the shaping and the shape are one. Both together see and exclaim:

> Ecce, Oxidia is the seed
> Dropped out of this amber-ember pod,
>
> Oxidia is the soot of fire,
> Oxidia is Olympia.

Olympia, the fire, the amber-ember pod, recalls "the greatness of poetry . . . the torches wisping in the underground
. . . the structure of vaults upon a point of light." In itself
it is something in the past. Oxidia, the soot, the seed, is a
world without shadows, where "Day is desire and night is
sleep" and the earth "is flat and bare." Here, finally, the two
are one in the man-poet Stevens's image of the man-poet, ordinary and extraordinary, lion and lute, monster and intelligence of the monster.

This synthesis, this *concordia discors,* the purpose and goal
of the poem, has evolved out of the opposition between that
ordinariness which seems to be without value and that poetic
extraordinariness which is essentially value itself. The struggle
originates out of the insistence of ordinary men that the poet
must sing them as they are in such a way as to affirm their
value and out of the poet's sense that, though he would like
to play serenades about things of obvious value, about heroes,
his true desire is to affirm value in things as they are. The
dialogue between the "I" and "they" occupies the first five
sections of the poem. The poet rather weakly says that he
tries to reach through the hero of his making to man, but that
he cannot quite do it, and that his music should be accepted
merely as "the serenade / Of a man that plays a blue guitar."
Spurred by the exclamation of III, the desire of men for a
poem which truly captures "man number one," the poet tries
out, in IV, a music which catches "A million people on one
string" and "all their manner in the thing." But, to the poet,
doing this is nothing like poetry; it does not sound heroic,
but "Like a buzzing of flies in autumn air." To sing of things
as they are is to abandon all sense of value, and the poet can
imagine such an abandonment only with disgust. The rousing
challenge of V, however, in which the people demand a heroic
effort from the poet, an impossible achievement,

Poetry

Exceeding music must take the place
Of empty heaven and its hymns,

Ourselves in poetry must take their place,
Even in the chattering of your guitar.

this challenge is too compelling, and, without another word
of protest, the poet accepts the challenge as his own. Thus, in
VI, the two, the I and the they, speak together their agreed-
upon-need. In truth, VI is the first pause, the first reconciliation, of "The Blue Guitar"; and it is an achieved pause, in
no way inconsistent with what precedes it, just the opposite of
being unprepared for. All agree: the blue guitar must be "the
place of things as they are" and the tune of the guitar must
be space, the only space there is from here to the end of the
poem. The dialogue between the I and the they thus cannot
continue, for the they are in the tune, their space is the tune,
and the I, of course, as player of the guitar, provides them
with the only place they can occupy. Being on the edge, being
isolated, is now impossible; as Stevens said, "I wanted to get
to the center," "I wanted to share the common life."

The wish, however, is not the deed, and from section VII
through XVI the poet moves from despair to despair as he
finds first one kind and then another of such shared commonness simply unendurable. He grants, in VII, that he can write
no more moon poetry, heroic poetry, great poetry of wisping
torches, and "the structure of vaults upon a point of light."
For "The moon shares nothing. It is a sea." It is pure blue,
cut off from all that is green. It is the very opposite of commonness; it is the "good, / The immaculate, the merciful
good, / Detached from us, from things as they are." Even
worse, as he considers men as they are, men with no value except what his tune gives them, he recognizes that even sun
poetry is forbidden him. Men seen as working in the sun are

96

unified by the sun, are given a center and value by the sun, and the fact that there is no such centrality outside the value-bestowing music of the guitar is the very condition which has joined the poetic I and common men in their effort to get along without "heaven and its hymns." Once cut off from the sun, however, "the earth is alive with creeping men, / Mechanical beetles never quite warm," and the poet concludes this section in despair: "The strings are cold on the blue guitar."

The space of the poet's tune, the place of his guitar, cannot rest any given order, any presupposed chain of being or hierarchy with either sun or moon as its pinnacle. Life in the space of this tune, as shown in VIII, is a storm, at best a movement of need and desire, from night to day, from darkness to light; the most the poet's "lazy, leaden twang" can do now is to be like "the reason in a storm"; it can strum out the anguish and the need, but no more. When the poet says: "I twang it out and leave it there," he is reverting to a despair like that of

> If to serenade almost to man
> Is to miss, by that, things as they are,
>
> Say that it is the serenade
> Of a man that plays a blue guitar.

Except that here his weakness is not that he can shape only images of value detached from man, but that he can shape man and his need of value, but without any sense of the value that is needed.

Settled gloom is what follows, in section IX. Men without value, with a need but no glimpse of what they need, such dullness the poet can evoke with ease. The "overcast blue / Of the air," the blue guitar, the thought of empty despair, the actor, his stage and its weather are all at one in the gloom of the space of the tune. To be sure, the poet senses the inadequacy of what he does; he cannot accept the idea that nothing

97

will come of nothing. Thus, he is "The maker of a thing yet to be made." Further, he feels that the very emptiness of the mood evoked is a bit grandiose, is pretentious and indulgent, like "silk / Sodden with his melancholy words." The dullness of loss depends on nostalgia for that which is lost.

In section X, a recovery of sorts is made. The poet, with some vigor, asserts that the hollows, the felt emptiness which made all melancholy, should be clapped full of tin. Then the poet, turned satirist, greets the latest secular hero, "A pagan in a varnished car." No one, as the strumming of the guitar reveals, believes in this pagan, though superficially all believe that all believe. The guitar performs its satiric function of toppling the hero from his prominence. What else could it do, given its commitment to see men as they are? Since, however, it topples all, it topples this one man

> Yet with a petty misery
> At heart, a petty misery

It is one thing to expose falseness in the hope of greeting the genuine, but quite another to expose it with the sense that absolutely nothing can stand intact against such exposure.

This petty misery, kept subordinate in X to the satiric hooing of the slick trombones, becomes the dominant feeling in XI, as the poet strums the chord which is the space of a world so miserable that men and even things become indistinguishable from their environment. In this chord, "all the flies are caught, / Wingless and withered, but living alive." Men as flies are men without value; that they are "living alive" implies their need and desire, their dissatisfaction with being trapped in such space. The very chord of overcast blue, that is, turns to discord because of insatiable desire, and Stevens concludes the section with the claim that there must be something deeper than this world of mere flux which could satisfy men's need:

> Deeper within the belly's dark
> Of time, time grows upon the rock.

What is "the rock"? Let us say, as XII says, that the rock is both guitar and its player:

> Tom-tom, c'est moi. The blue guitar
> And I are one.

Such arrogant self-deification cannot even be asserted without embarrassment. "The State, it is I" thus is asserted under the cover of a French phrase. Men are mere flies, wingless and withered; when they dance, however, even though shuffling, even though in chains, they become "High as the hall" because of their desire, because of their feeling for value. This feeling is made real by the music played by the orchestra; this music, in turn, is created by "his breath that lies awake at night," by the solitary guitarist who is his guitar, by the creative artist whose tune is space. The hard-headed guitarist, however, cannot rest content with this pretentious identification between himself and all the men heightened by his music. He accepts the logic but not the feeling of such grandiosity.

There may, in section XIII, be a solution in self-abnegation, in a notion of purely impersonal poetry.

> The pale intrusions into blue
> Are corrupting pallors

It is the idea that the poet himself is deified in his central, creative poetry that is corruptive. If one can be content to be obliterated in his music, to sacrifice himself utterly to the music, so that each creator simply becomes

> The unspotted imbecile revery,
> The heraldic center of the world
>
> Of blue, blue sleek with a hundred chins,
> The amorist Adjective aflame. . . .

99

then possibly the poet can accept value-laden poetry without the corrupting suggestion that his pale, little ego thus becomes divinely creative.

What sort of space is evoked by such a self-abnegatory conception of creation? It is a world of innumerable originative centers, each its own source and world, each "both star and orb." (XIV) Indeed, each creative center, whether a German chandelier or even a mere candle, creates its own light and space. Such a glorification of creativity at the expense of all creators is quite unsatisfactory, however. Before, men had been mere flies but at least the individual poet had been of value. Now, in a world of pluralistic creative centers, even the creators have lost their value as individuals. The I of the poet, as viewed in the chiaroscuro of space defined by his candle, is destroyed, he is "a man that is dead / At a table on which the food is cold." (XV) He is merely part of a painting in which his blood, as mere color, cannot be distinguished from wine.

Such disembodied love, that is, is an abandonment of all men as bodily individuals, is an abandonment of the earth as mother of all, and the earth avenges itself in its abandoned state as mere stone. (XVI) Love must be personal, must be bodily, must be earthly. Conceived in the skyey fashion of XIV, it turns earthly life into war in which each creative center, its person dead, wars against all others as a mere "chopping" of "the sullen psaltery." Physical lovers, once the earth is turned to stone, once love and earth are dissociated, may try

> To improve the sewers in Jerusalem,
> To electrify the nimbuses

but such efforts are a mockery of their desire. No, in their despair they are advised to

> Place honey on the altars and die,
> You lovers that are bitter at heart.

100

In section XVII Stevens affirms positively what was implicit negatively in XVI. The individual and his spirit, the force of his desires, must be at one. The person has a bodily mold. The only shape possible for his spirit, which is not "the soul, the mind," which is not some creative center "both star and orb," must be "the blue guitar." The blue guitar must be the mold of the spirit, as "a worm composing on a straw" is the mold of the north wind blowing. Thus, and only thus, are the person as body and his spirit, his anima, his animal, at one. In this way his dream, his desire, the blowing of his spirit, may become adequate to his body, may be at one with it. (XVIII) Only "After long strumming on certain nights" are spirit and body at one, and the guitar

> Gives the touch of the senses, not of the hand,
>
> But the very senses as they touch
> The wind-gloss.

Spirit becomes bodily and body becomes spiritual in this, one of the most delicate of images to be found in the poem:

> Or as daylight comes,
>
> Like light in a mirroring of cliffs,
> Rising upward from a sea of ex.

The light rises from who knows where, from "a sea of ex," from the mysterious nothing that shares nothing with us, and becomes one with "things as they are," with the cliffs, but in such a way that the spirit, the light, is at one with the stone in the vital movement of "a mirroring of cliffs." One's awareness is a touching much as the wind's blowing is a touching in the phrase "The wind-gloss." The "mirroring of cliffs" picks up its movement and vitality as "gloss" works upon and becomes one with "mirroring" so that the mere movement of

101

light on cliffs is felt to be the wind moving over and glossing the rock, and this is at one with the working of one's senses as they touch the wind in movement. Nowhere else does Stevens capture the spirituality of the physical or the physicality of the spiritual more exquisitely. The unreality and spectral quality of the lights of XIV and XV and the stoniness of the earth in XVI are miraculously overcome as the poet's dream becomes a thing adequate to its object, as the mold of the guitar becomes adequate to the mold of the person.

In section XIX Stevens affirms as his aspiration what he has just imagined with such sensuous immediacy. He would reduce the body, the monster, the object, things as they are, to himself and, as guitarist, as lutanist, as poet, simply be the intelligence of the monster. He would, that is, turn mere body into the body as it exists beyond itself, as it exists in its most exquisite feelings. As Stevens said to Hi Simons: the poet must "express people beyond themselves, because that is exactly the way they are. Their feelings demonstrate the subtlety of people."[13] If the poet could do that, then he would be "the lion in the lute / Before the lion locked in stone." His basic problem is to be both lion and lute, both ordinary man and exceptional poet, "the two together as one."

Can the poet believe in his capacity to realize this aspiration? His need to believe, his uncertainty, is the subject of XX. He is asking of himself something far more difficult than he has previously imagined as the job of the poet, To be a substitute for the moon or the sun; to be the very creator of value for all men: such ideas surely sound presumptuous enough for any poet to utter as his possible task. But here Stevens is suggesting that he must be both the center of value and the very men of no faith whose value he would create. He must be both lute and lion, god and carpenter, and both at the same time. Can he believe such an idea? It is no wonder that, in XX, he thinks of "believe" as a force outside himself and his guitar, as "a brother full / Of love" with whom he could be at one only by some miracle. Before such a demand, his guitar indeed seems fragile, a mere "worm composing on a straw." And he shakes his head in disbelief: "Poor pale, poor pale guitar." To bring those "pale intrusions into blue" in such a way that they would not be "corrupting pallors," to be "The heraldic center of the world" and yet remain one's common self, to be poet and insurance executive (Who, Wally?), this is hardly something to be bruited about casually on an ordinary evening in New Haven or in Hartford.

The problem of "believe," however, is not so serious at this stage in the development of the poem as it was earlier, so that the sad despair of XX can be swept away by the grand "as if" of XXI. Stevens no longer thinks of the poet as an entity, a form of being, distinct from things as they are. Mere supposal, mere play, mere intelligence, is all that the poet need be, now that he accepts his oneness with the monster. His belief in himself as poet is a belief in that aspect of himself that is unreal, and this is at one with his disbelief in that aspect of himself as real. As mere man, as an ordinary self, he is at one with the men that live in the land and with the land, the earth itself, with Chocorua and the mountains of one's land,

> Without shadows, without magnificence,
> The flesh, the bone, the dirt, the stone.

As the lute containing the lion, as the intelligence of the monster, not as a reified self like the discarded sun, "that gold self aloft," as pure unreality like the shadow of oneself and of the mountain Chocorua, as mere play, as the playing of the guitar, the poet is "A substitute for all the gods," is "lord of the land and lord / Of the men that live in the land, high lord." And, worked out as mere supposal, as a "perhaps," in XXII, the poet affirms "the universal intercourse" between "The flesh, the bone, the dirt, the stone" which are the poetic subject of his poem and such objects outside the poem, in reality; he affirms the universal intercourse between "the lion in the lute" and "the lion locked in stone." If, that is, the poet makes his own mere manliness the subject of his poem, then he can rightly suppose that mere men may take from his poem a sense of themselves suffused with echoes of the lute, may live locked in stone but as if freed and valuable in the strumming of the lute.

From the firmness of this achievement, in XXI and XXII, the poet then sweeps with unflagging exuberance through the final eleven sections of the poem. He shifts from a section emphasizing the lute to a section emphasizing the stone and back again; but the two are one, the lion is present whether as subject of the poem or as part of reality, whether in Olympia or Oxidia, because "the universal intercourse" between the two, as play and thought, has been achieved beyond the fear of loss. XXIII is all song, is Dichtung, is eternal music, containing however the real, Wahrheit, the grunted breath of the undertaker, whose business of course has to do with mere, mortal men. XXIV concentrates on the real world, on mud, and on a young scholar living in it. The action of the section, however, is the scholar's finding a poem "like a missal" in the mud; and at least some part of that poem, some Olympic, Latined phrase, serves as "A hawk of life," an accurate vision of mud which gives it value, which is redemptive, which lifts bestiality into song. In XXV Stevens shifts the emphasis to the imaginative as the point on which the whole real world turns. It is not, however, a still point because the poet, even when so exultant in his creativity as the very act which makes the world move and mean, is still an animal, conceived as a kind of circus seal which "held the world upon his nose."

The next two sections, XXVI and XXVII, are built out of a common imagery, the land as real and the sea as imaginative. Having achieved a reconciliation of the two, Stevens no longer imagines the sea as alien, as that which shares nothing with

us. Even in his wildest flights, the poet always begins and ends
at the real; and, in the middle, when soaring in the clouds, he
must contend with the "Sand heaped in the clouds," and
must struggle by way of his alphabet with the indestructible
earth giant. Even his most comical acrobatics, that is, must be
attuned to the ordinary, to the grunting of the undertaker, to
that fat thumb that beats out ai-yi-yi. Or, as in XXVII, even in
the winter of the earth, when all is gloom and men are snow-
men, when all seems solidified and objectified, when the lion is
frozen in stone, one must recognize the presence of the imagination, the presence of the sea as it "drifts through the winter
air." If the sea were not recognized as the very source of this
gloom, as congealed in "the icicles on the eaves," if its movement were not felt in this stasis, then the sea would be a
"form of ridicule," its movement would mock the stillness of
the winter scene. And, likewise, its own icebergs, its own solid
shapes, would be a satire on its own endless motion, on "The
demon that cannot be himself" but is ever changing in his
unreality.

In section XXVIII Stevens's imagination is most philosophical. He will not be caught in any form of sensational or empirical solipsism. The world, he thinks, is really there and as
ordinary man he lives as a native in it. What he sees is truly
there as he sees it; this is his thought, but his thought is
not part of a mind existing as an entity above and beyond the
world as seen. On the other hand, Stevens is no naive realist,
for he knows that things are there as they are, "the wave / In
which the watery grasses flow," because he thinks of them as
really there; thus he must add, as if it stems from his thought
and will, that the watery grasses "are fixed as a photograph."
The world is as it is and as the poet sees it, because he thinks
it is as it is, because of this very present movement of his
thought. Section XXIX pushes this thought to an even higher
level of understanding. Here he affirms, in this living movement of the present, at the high level of unreal, imaginative

105

play, the thought that every structure of thought, that every shaped system of thought, that even the most ample cathedral built to balance harmoniously with the things outside it, is always, as seen from the unreal imagination, a little out of balance. "The bells are the bellowing of bulls." Yes and no. They contain and they omit. Beyond the finest thought, in the "perhaps" and "as if" of the imagination, the poet sees the falseness of the Franciscan don's fictive cathedral and yet the rightness of his fiction, the rightness of his effort to realize a balance between his structure and the structure of reality. It is the coincidence of one's effort to achieve such a balance and his knowledge that he never quite achieves it that brings together and reconciles things as they are and the playful imagination.

Given this reconciliation of the struggle for finality and the absence of absolute finality, given this position so close to the absolute historicism of Benedetto Croce, a form of neo-idealism much closer, in its aesthetic sensitivity, to realism than any Anglo-American naturalism, pragmatism, or realism has ever been, Stevens can move confidently into the climactic section, the thirtieth section, in which he sets forth the oneness of ordinary man and extraordinary poet, and affirms "Oxidia is Olympia."

The poet's achievement, "The rhapsody of things as they are" (XXXI), is beyond both absolute idealism, with its "lark fixed in the mind, / In the museum of the sky," and dialectical materialism, organized as it is around the contention of employer and employee. He knows that the sun bubbling up, the "Spring sparkle and the cock-bird shriek" cannot touch the employer and employee; he knows there is no elemental necessity linking the two worlds; he knows they are not unified by an absolute idea, any sun in the sky. But he knows he can create and unify even such a day of dispersed, logically unrelated incidents by his imaginative playing. In this world

"The Man with the Blue Guitar"

> Morning is not sun,
> It is this posture of the nerves,
>
> As if a blunted player clutched
> The nuances of the blue guitar.

Indeed, in XXXII, he welcomes just this unorganized world of contingencies, a world free of "the rotted names," a world unreduced to cathedral or to any established system of thought and belief. Out of such darkness, with every crust of shape destroyed, he discovers and glories in "the madness of space" and its "jocular procreations."

Only as lutanist, as guitarist, as poet, can one contain all the sensuous selves with all their sensuous worlds, all systems and all their utopias, without being reduced to any, but also without reducing any of them to less than what they really are. One does not contain the brass world within one's own golden world. One contains both brass and gold only as a shadow, only as their poetic intelligence. As a man Stevens chose an "up-to-date capitalism" as against communism; as a man he struggled contradictorily between a primal sympathy for the oppressed Abyssinians and a sense that Mussolini's effort to colonize their country resembled England's efforts to colonize the America of the Indians, efforts which he could not condemn as evil.[14] As a man he was ordinary, uncertain, often confused. As a man commenting on his own poems, he was astute and helpful, but cautious and modest and even pedestrian. When the ordinary man became poet, however, he was magnificent. He contained within himself as Olympic all the Oxidic elements which as mere man he both affirmed and opposed. His most marvelous extravagance, moreover, lies in his scrupulous refusal to abandon or to beautify falsely the plain stoniness of his and our ordinary natures. Nor does such poetic magnificence permit us any critical modesty. It demands that we press all our ordinary "rotted names" into the service of a criticism adequate in its discursiveness to his poetic greatness, a criticism that balances his poetry in its living moment of thought just because, hawk that it must be, this criticism never rests content with any of its neat formulations, just because it too moves in the darkness of the "jocular procreations" that occur in the space that is the tune that is played on the blue guitar by this finally unobjectifiable poet.

5

"Notes toward a Supreme Fiction"

If "Notes toward a Supreme Fiction" is the great poem so many readers have felt it to be, then it must have an inner action that justifies its length and makes all its parts significant, however diverse they may be. At the same time, its parts, even its very lines, must have a richness, a density, a texture, a quality beyond mere verbality, that holds the reader and compels him to dwell upon them, to savor them pleasurably, with the delight that all poetic detail provides.

Numerous efforts have been made recently to sum up the sense of the "Notes."[1] The state of present criticism concerning this poem may itself, I think, be summed up as attentive to the whole at the expense of the details of the poem. Even the efforts of summary themselves have, however, been inadequate because they have, by and large, failed to show that there is genuine development in the poem. Attention has been unduly limited to the philosophical problems in the poem, especially to the epistemological problem, the relationship between object and subject, nature and man, reality and imagination, things as they are and fictive things.

The main difficulty in such interpretations lies in the fact that Stevens affirms his solution to the problem at the beginning of the poem, so that he really has no place to go. Thus, near the end of the poem, when he exclaims ecstatically:

> That's it: the more than rational distortion,
> The fiction that results from feeling. Yes, that.
>
> They will get it straight one day at the Sorbonne.
> We shall return at twilight from the lecture
> Pleased that the irrational is rational
>
> (III. x, p. 406)

one cannot but recall that the same basic thing was being affirmed at the very beginning of the poem (I, iii). The point is that the whole world, from its first idea to its slightest detail, is seen as it is only by him who loves it, who sees it with feeling. Seen with feeling, seen with love, poetically, imaginatively, the world, from its littlest bees and violets to its ordinary men, its presidents and canons and captains and maidens and widows, is a distortion of the world as seen rationally. But irrational sight and thought are in truth more rational than reason. "The fiction that results from feeling" is the real thing. The world is seen and thought in its purity, in its candor, in its immaculate form, only by him who sees and thinks it with feeling. This is where the poem arrives. But it is also where the poem begins. Thus, Stevens says that, poetically,

> We move between these poles:
> From that ever-early candor to its late plural
>
> And the candor of them is the strong exhilaration
> Of what we feel from what we think, of thought
> Beating in the heart, as if blood newly came,

110

An elixir, an excitation, a pure power.

(I. iii, p. 382)

In other words, the first idea and its whole world in all its multiplicity are identical with the feelings of one who thinks them, of one who thinks them with feeling, so that his thought beats in his heart. In comments on "The Blue Guitar" Stevens said that people as they are are really their feelings, and that their feelings are beyond them, are in the outer world.[2] Hence the poet was right to play the people, on his guitar, as they are, but beyond themselves. Here, in the "Notes," is the same idea, presented as initial supposition and as triumphant conclusion. If that is what the "Notes" is all about, with its subordinate corollaries concerning pleasure and change, if the poem is really a study in epistemology, then obviously it can have no significant development. It ends where it begins. Between "that ever-early candor" and "its late plural," all that Stevens has done is to weave associational variations on this rather dogmatically held belief in imagination as reality, in beauty as truth.

In an earlier attempt to capture the whole of the "Notes"— with a neglect of details which I intend to remedy in this chapter—I sought out the inner propulsion, movement, and development of the poem in Stevens's effort to reconcile the exceptional poet with ordinary men, an effort similar to, but distinct from, that of "The Man with the Blue Guitar."[3] I argued that from a monotonal beginning in the first idea, Stevens gradually splits off from the first idea the major abstraction, the idea of man, the commonal, and a second abstraction, major man, the poet who is an expedient of the first abstraction, an exponent, who would make, confect, a final elegance by plainly propounding the nature of the first abstraction, of ordinary men. Further, I suggested that in the second part of the poem the gap between ordinary men and extraordinary poet is widened. We can have, on the one hand,

111

a name and an image for ordinary man: he is the man "In that old coat, those sagging pantaloons," and he is to be found "Looking for what was, where it used to be." He seeks permanence, he ordains the bee to be immortal. The poet, on the other hand, thrives on change and sees its ironical presence even where ordinary men are insisting on permanence. Finally, I found that in the third part of the poem Stevens brings the two abstractions back together as a *concordia discors,* as an identity of opposites. Ordinary men impose orders according to their desires; the poet discovers orders out of his desire, his love. Both, in other words, make fictions out of feeling; the fictions of ordinary men are impositions; those of the poet are discoveries; but both are "The fiction that results from feeling." Ordinary men eschew change, they impose orders to "stop the whirlwind, balk the elements." Though the poet revels in change, Stevens at last discovers in him a repetitiousness, a permanence, and out of this discovery he is enabled to imagine the supreme fiction, the fiction of an absolute, an archdiscoverer, an angel "Serenely gazing at the violent abyss." What gives permanence to the poet and thus, at last, permits an image of his inner power as angel, an image comparable to that previously set forth for ordinary man, is the repetition of his act of discovering the way ordinary men endlessly impose orders according to their desires. Unlike ordinary men, the poet alone is "of repetition most master," because he alone is not only repetitious but has also discovered a form of repetition that is endlessly various, that is, the act of discovering the essential order in the efforts of ordinary men to impose order. Thus, I had concluded, Stevens reconciled the exceptional poet and ordinary men; he found an identity in their diversity and imaginatively affirmed it without sacrificing the diversity.

I have been puzzled that other critics ignored the distinction in the poem between the poet, between MacCullough, and ordinary men, especially because, in my opinion, only by recognizing it can one sense the immense struggle and development

112

in the poem which makes it so extraordinary an achievement. Evidence for the distinction is overpowering. When Stevens affirms that the first idea is an imagined thing and first suggests an image of the poetic spirit itself, the "giant prone in violet space," which he says may be the MacCullough, he then goes on to say that "the MacCullough is MacCullough": that is, the principle, the abstract, of the poet is at one with the individual poet, in his singular, as particular (I, viii). But he then—and this is my point—insists that "It does not follow that major man is man," that is, it is not also true that the singular poet is the same as an ordinary man. Further, he then declares that one should not give a name or an image to the major man because "The hot of him is purest in the heart"; whereas, in the very next section, he provides an image of man that all can and do and should see:

> in his old coat,
> His slouching pantaloons, beyond the town,
>
> Looking for what was, where it used to be
> (I. x)

Nor does Stevens, at any point, reject this image as he has just rejected the image of the MacCullough, the giant.

There are, however, two reasons for neglecting or even denying the distinction, and these I ignored in my previous study. First, and simplest, Stevens uses "major" in reference both to man and poet. The major abstraction from the first idea is the idea of man and this idea is the commonal (I, ix). Major man, in contrast to the major abstraction, the idea of man, is distinctive, an exponent of the major abstraction. Stevens, it seems to me, uses "major" in reference to both, because he wishes to convey the very sense of distinguishing them; he strives to catch the feeling of the thought that draws the two apart out of oneness. Though he wishes to make the distinction, he at the same time wishes to suggest the oneness from which they diverge. Thus, their distinctness is not simply obvious and, unless one is alert to the underlying, shaping action of the poem, it could easily be missed.

Second and more important, Stevens thinks, as all should know even without *The Necessary Angel* as confirmation, that we all live by the imagination and thus are all, to an extent, artists.[4] MacCullough, Franz Hals, the ephebe, the poet referred to in the poem, and Stevens, who with his speaking voice makes the poem, all these are major men, are men of imagination. But ordinary men too, the president, Canon Aspirin, Nanzia Nunzio and Ozymandias, the blue woman, linked and lacquered, all these who are of the commonal live by the imagination too. As a result, one is likely to insist that all are identical or, more reasonably, that differences between ordinary men, between extraordinary men, and those between extraordinary men and ordinary men, that these differences are not themselves significantly different. Previously I had laid emphasis on the point that, although all these figures are the same in the sense that they make fictions out of their feelings, the fictions of the extraordinary are discoveries whereas those of the ordinary are impositions. Although I still believe this distinction to be crucial, I now see that it has a foundation beyond itself. This foundation, indeed, is the element most frequently emphasized by other critics: it is the non-human, which includes a first idea, a heaven that has expelled us and our images, a world of red emptiness, of clouds, a muddy center, and lions, elephants, bears, and birds that respond to those nonhuman forces with immediacy and in complete oneness with them. It is in reference to this world, in fact, that the difference between men and major man takes on its significance most clearly. This world is dominated by time and by dissolution. Animals live in harmony with it:

> The bear,
> The ponderous cinnamon, snarls in his mountain

114

At summer thunder and sleeps through winter snow.

(I. v)

Men, in contrast, are bred against this world and its first idea, with its endless flux and dissolution. By means of their imaginations they make fictions to endure, to be of value as only the lasting can be. They roof themselves in against the flux, they concentrate on what was, where it used to be, on endurance. The Italian girls with jonquils in their hair are doing just what their mothers did. The Canon Aspirin "establishes statues of reasonable men" in the corridors of the capitals he has made. "It is a brave affair." Furthermore, they impose order and permanence on the ever-changing non-human world itself. They remake animals, they "lash the lion, / Caparison elephants, teach bears to juggle." Like Eve, they make air a mirror of themselves; they make the place in which they live dependent on themselves.

These fictions, of course, are clearly false. The poet, the major man, the man of central imagination whose fictions are discoveries, is the one who recognizes their falsity. He is the one who recognizes that we live in a place that is not our own and that "The air is not a mirror but bare board." He it is who hears the abysmal instruments of nature making "sounds like pips / Of the sweeping meanings that we add to them." He knows that nature mocks us by undermining even our finest academies; he beholds them "like structures in a mist," as phantasmal, as unreal, as "False flick, false form." He is not, however, merely a nature poet. He does not identify himself with the mocking force of nature and simply expose man's folly. Shelley's effort to identify himself with the west wind is echoed here:

Be thou me, said sparrow, to the crackled blade,
And you and you, be thou me as you blow,
When in my coppice you behold me be.

(II. vi)

115

and it strikes Stevens as idiot minstrelsy. There is not enough change in ever-changing nature. What impresses major man is the immense variety, the significant change, in man's heroic efforts to impose fixed forms on nature. He recognizes that seasonal changes, the shift from winter to spring, the return of the bee and the hyacinths, are boring in their recurrence. True human change, heroic change, is the synthesis of opposites, the synthesis of recurrent, natural change and the individual efforts of men to fix shapes of value. For the poet it is not the fixed shapes that are of value, but the endlessly varying efforts of man to fix shapes against the drifting waste of nature. He is at one with nature in seeing it as it is; he is at one with men in recognizing not only the truth that their fictions are false but also the value, the heroism, of their fictive efforts. Ordinary men, imposing as always, strive to make not only air but even animals over in their own images. The poet, in contrast, would simply have ordinary men be aware of the affirmative truthfulness of the poet concerning their falseness. With such a oneness in difference, with such mutual love, the poet can then affirm, with earned serenity:

> How simply the fictive hero becomes the real;
> How gladly with proper words the soldier dies,
> If he must, or lives on the bread of faithful speech.
> (Epilogue)

The soldier dies without illusions but without despair, because the poet, speaking truly, has affirmed the illusoriness of the soldier's fictions and the value of his fictive efforts.

Such a reading accounts, I believe, for the major forces in the poem, emphasizes the immense struggle that goes on among them as the poem develops, and explains the complexity and unity of its final reconciliation. Its value, even so, is quite limited. It indicates that the poem is an action, not a product; it suggests that the poem expands, unified by an inner propulsion, and, thus, is not merely a joining of scheme and revery, of an arbitrary framework and clusters of association. It insists that the poem has a serious meaning and that the meaning is individual, not a group of ideas Stevens shared with this philosopher or that. It does not, however, indicate much about the poetic significance of the poem, and doing that is a major obligation of criticism.

I

Poetically, the challenge of the "Notes" for Stevens is to make the visible real by imagining it as suffused by, as at one with, the invisible. This means that he would be a poet of the sublime, but in the special sense that he would fuse the sublime, that which is beyond our imagery, with our imagery, with things as we see them. It means that he would be an inspired poet, but in the special sense that the muse, the inspiring force, the poetic spirit, would be at one with the individual man as poet.

In other words, to read "Notes toward a Supreme Fiction" poetically, one must recognize that the poet shaping the poem is not only an individual poet, a man who can write letters felicitously and ingratiatingly, but is also the impossible possible philosophers' man. For Stevens, in this poem, is in the tradition of poets set forth by C. M. Bowra in his *Inspiration and Poetry*. One reads the poem with the *Ion* and *On the Sublime* in the background, with a sense that Stevens could have made a fourth subject in John Arthos's book on the sublime, *Dante Michelangelo Milton*. When Stevens says, of the poet's inspiriting force, of "The pensive giant prone in violet space," of that "leaner being moving in on him, / Of greater aptitude and apprehension,"

> Yet look not at his colored eyes. Give him
> No names. Dismiss him from your images.
> The hot of him is purest in the heart.
>
> (I. viii)

117

one thinks of Coleridge's lines on the figure of the inspired poet:

> And all should cry, Beware! Beware!
> His flashing eyes, his floating hair!
> Weave a circle round him thrice,
> And close your eyes with holy dread,
> For he on honey-dew hath fed,
> And drunk the milk of Paradise.

Or, even more appropriately, when one thinks of the lines that indicate clearly that Love is the heart of the poem: "And for what, except for you, do I feel love"; and, in reference to the force of inspiration, "he that reposes / On a breast forever precious for that touch"; and, of lines concerning the object of the poet's love, "Fat girl, terrestrial, my summer, my night" and "You / become the soft-footed phantom, the irrational / Distortion, however fragrant, however dear," one may recall Dante's

> I' mi son un, che quando
> Amor mi spira, noto, e a quel modo
> ch' è detto dentro vo significando.[5]

At the same time, there is a crucial difference between Stevens and these inspired and sublime poets of the past. Dante's poetic problem, in the *Paradiso,* is to imagine the unimaginable, to make the reader experience that which is above, beyond, and outside images. He does this by putting himself into the other-world and having the blessed take a form and a place just for him; and he puts light to endlessly varied uses in order to suggest a super-light. He distorts and transforms both what we see and what we cannot see in order to suggest the truly real world, the supernatural world of heaven. Shakespeare stays closer to the world as ordinarily experienced, even in his most abstract play, *The Winter's Tale.* He strives to evoke the invisible, quintessential pattern of human experience by having events of that play succeed each other so abruptly and so arbitrarily that the audience is shaken out of its common stance, from which it views the world, and cast into the more inclusive sphere, the truly real world, in which the real and the imagined, the visible and the invisible, the fanciful nothing that causes Leontes' jealousy and the terrible consequences of that very real jealousy, occur with equal force. The pattern, of course, dominates and the ordinary world is transformed into the extraordinary, the unlikely, which we are made to feel as inexorably necessary.

In our epoch, however, the idea of a transcendent world, a world detached from and beyond us, an invisible world to be imagined only in visual terms, cannot be taken seriously. There is only this world which we experience and as we experience it. Stevens accepts this world, which is "neither heaven nor hell," and strives to convey the invisible lurking just behind every visibility, "A seeing and unseeing in the eye," the action of one's spirit which is a kind of shadow to every bodily image.

To accomplish such a thing in our time, however, is no small task. As a commonalty, we live in a dualistic world composed of the cinematically immediate and the technologically abstract. We watch our astronauts sail through space on television and know that it is half of the real; the other half is made up of the technical operations of the brains behind the scene. It is a very practical world bringing together and, in a way, debasing the British tradition of sensationalism and the French tradition of rationalism. Of poetry like that of Stevens's, the earthily oriented critic will lament its abstractness. British critics, nourished on an empirical tradition, find the conceptual activity in Stevens's poems quite unreal and enjoy contrasting it to the sensuous immediacy of D. H. Lawrence.[6] The American version of this criticism appears in Randall Jarrell's insistence, against Stevens, that the poet must always concentrate on the time and place in which we are. Karl Shapiro will gruffly dismiss Stevens as having no imagination at all.[7] Indeed, what else could he say, given the way he has taken the most sensual poetry of our tradition, that of Whitman, and, in *The Bourgeois Poet,* turned it into prose, driving it even further into the surfaces of our sensual mediocrity. On the other hand, a critic like Yvor Winters, committed to rationalism and to the poetry of Valéry as supreme, cannot but find poems like the "Notes" too vague and fuzzy.[8]

Stevens lived his whole life as an ordinary American, but with a fastidiousness derivative from his absorption in French culture. As a poet, however, he overcame this dualism of the sensuously immediate and the technologically abstract. With no direct influence to be claimed at all, one may say that his sense of the ultimacy of the felt, the passionate movement of the mind, make his poetry seem closest to the tradition of great Italian poetry, the poetry of Foscolo, Leopardi, D'Annunzio, Pascoli, Ungaretti, and Montale. This may, in part, explain the effectiveness of Renato Poggioli's translations of poems by Stevens into Italian and also the sensitiveness of Glauco Cambon's criticism of Stevens's poetry. I must admit that cultural placement of this kind cannot be pushed very far. It represents something a little too personal on my part, something more like an imposition than a discovery. It may, nonetheless, help the reader keep his footing and proceed cautiously as he considers my comments on the "Notes" itself.

The first section of the poem illustrates my basic point. It combines a single, intensely pure image with a series of high abstractions which concludes with the most abstract of all words, *be.*

> The sun
> Must bear no name, gold flourisher, but be
> In the difficulty of what it is to be.

The image and the abstractions, however, are fused in the

style of the poem, in the style of an inspired poet who would have us see an image as both visible and invisible, with "A seeing and unseeing in the eye." The problem of shaping a pure image poetically is not a new one for Stevens. He fails at it in "The Man on the Dump" and his failure is a crucial part of the achievement of that poem:

> and the moon comes up as the moon
> (All its images are in the dump) and you see
> As a man (not like an image of a man),
> You see the moon rise in the empty sky.

And he joshes at the pedagogue, in a "Study of Two Pears," who would see the pears as resembling nothing else. But here in the "Notes" (as later in the thirtieth section of "An Ordinary Evening in New Haven") he triumphs in his effort:

> How clean the sun when seen in its idea,
> Washed in the remotest cleanliness of a heaven
> That has expelled us and our images . . .

He makes these three lines into the experience of a pure image by means of his style, indirectly. As is usual with Stevens, his concern in this section is not simply with the image as it is in itself; it is with the difficulty of seeing it as it is in itself. He begins the poem by giving general directions as to how the first idea is to be perceived, and he does it, even from the start, in such a way as to make us squint.

> Begin, ephebe, by perceiving the idea
> Of this invention

The "the" and "this" suggest that we ought to know what he is talking about, but, of course, we do not, and so we knit our brows. He then specifies, as in apposition: he means "this invented world" and "The inconceivable idea of the sun." Now we know. But what we know is more baffling than our initial ignorance. "This invented world"? One can only be ignorant of that. Surely "this world" is not invented; or, if it is an invented world we are to think of, it clearly is not "this invented world." As for perceiving an idea that is inconceivable, well, such a distinction between perceiving and conceiving, presented without analysis, is most puzzling and one totters over an abyss of epistemological recollections. Stevens intends just such bafflement.

In the next stanza, as if saying the simplest of things, he asserts that, for such perceiving, the needed knowledge is of how to "become an ignorant man again." He is, indeed, being most helpful. We are already so baffled (unless we are falsely pouring all sorts of illicit, extrinsic meanings into the lines) as to be losing all our systemic learnings (which, of course, means that we are becoming ignorant men).

> You must become an ignorant man again
> And see the sun again with an ignorant eye
> And see it clearly in the idea of it.

The form of the stanza suggests that he is becoming more and more specific, clarifying a first generalization with more precise statements. But the fact that he is really just repeating himself with minor variations works to cancel out the apparent clarification. "Ignorant," "sun," "idea," "see," and "again" are simply repeated, and "eye" adds nothing to "perceive" and "clearly" clears up nothing.

Ephebe is then told, in the third stanza, not to do things it would never have occurred to us to do, at least in this context; not to suppose or compose an inventing mind, of "A voluminous master folded in his fire," as source of the idea of the sun. Such forbidden suppositions are most nebulous, are even anti-images. They are nebulous not simply because forbidden, and not merely because unrealized, but mainly

because presented in a way that calls attention to its rhetoric
(Never suppose . . . nor for that) and to its sound and tone
(suppose . . . compose; an inventing mind . . . for that
mind; A voluminous master folded in his fire). In sum, this
stanza, like the first two, though all about the need for clear
perception, is pure sound (especially with so many words repeated) and intellectual confusion (because the words repeated
do not take on added meaning).

Only in the fourth stanza does Stevens break free of the
heavy, repetitious, didactic rhetoric of the section, and he
does so with a sigh of relief:

> How clean the sun when seen in its idea

as if he is himself expelling from his mind the artifice of the
first three stanzas. We squint with him and we truly see, as he
says, in lines that sweep rhythmically (in direct opposition to
the heavy hammering that precedes) with

> Washed in the remotest cleanliness of a heaven
> That has expelled us and our images . . .

What do we see? The rhythmical sweep of the lines makes us
sweep with our eyes the sky, as if at one with a washing, cleans-
ing, whitening movement that takes us to the remotest point
beyond us. And, then, looking as intensely as we can, seeing
nothing of our selves or of our images, we see, we almost see,
we see and unsee, with "A seeing and unseeing in the eye,"
something very like a pale white disc, that luminous sphere
that is the supreme good seen by the Socratic mystic.

A squinting glimpse is all we are given, but for a moment,
in the central of our being, we experience a vivid transparence
that is peace. Thereafter, and to the end of the section, Stevens
smears and smudges everything by rhetorical repetition and
tonal thickness (Let purple Phoebus . . . Let Phoebus; umber

harvest . . . autumn umber; lie . . . die; Phoebus . . . ephebe;
A name . . . named; There was a project . . . There is a
project; but be . . . to be). It is a cloudy, muddy poem, with
only the one breakthrough into utter purity. The breakthrough does not occur as a miracle, however, but as a result
of the immense poetic action taking place. There is a poetic
giant, the MacCullough, sweeping the heavens clean so that
we may see; there is a beau linguist using words in such a
way that we can imagine the first idea. We do not see him,
but we feel him, "The hot of him is purest in the heart."

Even the first idea, however, is seen very much as we see an
ordinary thing, the sun when most remote and self-contained,
on a winter day. Further, the next sections of the "Notes" are
dedicated to showing that, through poetry, we can see everything with a purity, a candor, a whiteness, like that in which
we saw the first idea. Bored with the world in parcels, as apart-
ments, we were sent back to its first idea. But once seen, in
the ravishments of its truth, that bores us too. We do not
wish to contemplate it in itself for more than a moment. Even
more, we do not wish to see the whole world as a hierarchy,
with each thing in its place, as determined by the first idea, as
an allegorical structure. We wish rather to turn back to the
particulars of the world and to see them as they are, yet somehow as suffused with the candid power of the first idea. This,
of course, is nonsense. Either one views particulars as mere
particles or one perceives them as part of a system topped by
the sun. But nonsense is just what the poem gives, just as
"Life's nonsense pierces us with strange relation." We concentrate, for instance, on the mere present, apart from all
system, and yet in poetry we see it suffused with candor:

> And still the grossest iridescence of ocean
> Howls hoo and rises and howls hoo and falls.

Or we think of a single detail of the past, and the same oc-

curs: "By day / The wood-dove used to chant his hoobla hoo."
Or we think of the future, on a moonlit night, and it too is
suffused by that immaculate nonsense of the first idea:

> At night an Arabian in my room,
> With his damned hoobla-hoobla-hoobla-how,
> Inscribes a primitive astronomy
>
> Across the unscrawled fores the future casts
> And throws his stars around the floor.

The moon as an Arabian? Was not the death of one god the
death of all? Was not Phoebus, the god of poetry, buried under autumn umber? Yes, when we contemplated the first idea.
But our interests are not merely mystical. We would experience the rich individuality of the parts of the world, both
human and nonhuman, with the exhilaration of mystical
contemplation. Thus, when in section VIII Stevens says:

> If MacCullough himself lay lounging by the sea,
>
> Drowned in its washes, reading in the sound,
> About the thinker of the first idea,
> He might take habit, whether from wave or phrase,
>
> Or power of the wave, or deepened speech,
> Or a leaner being, moving in on him,
> Of greater aptitude and apprehension,
>
> As if the waves at last were never broken,
> As if the language suddenly, with ease,
> Said things it had laboriously spoken.
> (I. viii, p. 387)

this figure who "lay lounging by the sea, / Drowned in its
washes" recalls that purple Phoebus who was left to "die in
autumn umber." But MacCullough is washed clean of autumn
umber by the waves of human passion and he speaks a lan-

guage that is human. He is a person and his action is personal. Not the god of poetry but a crystal hypothesis, a force that is real, that is a force only as it works in an individual poet, is the "leaner being, moving in on him." We can say of the MacCullough that he may be, that he is an abstraction, a principle, in himself: we can say that he is, that he becomes actual, only as "swaddled" in the revery of an individual poet. The poet is both the MacCullough and MacCullough, both principle and particle, and he is born and reborn only as actual poems are written. Major man, the poet, then, is a "foundling of the infected past." He is not a myth as pure idea, he is not Phoebus; he is born recurrently of that non-human poetic power, that principle, and the infected particle that is an individual man responsive to the waves of human passion and agile with human speech. And one cannot say that the principle itself is the cause of the poem. When Mac-Cullough becomes poetic, it may be because of the "power of the wave, or deepened speech, / Or a leaner being, moving in on him / Of greater aptitude and apprehension." Such a faith does not seem amenable to "reason's click-clack, its applied / Enflashings." It is poetic and real, part of the world in which "Life's nonsense pierces us with strange relation" and "the irrational is rational."

II

Just as the poet of the "Notes" turns away from the idea of the sun to enjoy the individual parts of the world, just as he can accept the spirit of poetry only as realized in individual poets, so the critic or reader of the "Notes" must turn from the essential action of the poem and from the poetic quality of the whole poem to enjoy the richness of its individual parts. Just as the formation of the corpus of a poet's work tempts one to concentrate on all the work at the expense of individual poems, so every long poem tempts one to treat of the whole while slighting its individual details. Yet it is evident that a great long poem is distinguished by the quality of its details, by the rhythms of its individual lines. Only because of them does one wish to take a poem within him on his breath and possess it in his heart.

Of all modern poets Stevens, I think, most forcefully reveals that we are untrained to hear voices in their individual rhythms and that we must overcome this insensitivity in order to appreciate genuine poetry. No area of criticism is so undeveloped today as the study of rhythm.[9] Even the few who have shown interest in the subject tend to shift their attention away from the rhythm of individual lines to the overall rhythm of a poem or a poet, or, even more dissipatingly, to the general subject of metrics. Even so sensitive a critic as Yvor Winters, beginning with an insistence upon the importance of poetic rhythm, very quickly confuses it with meter and reduces it to meter and its variations. The aspect of criticism most in need of development today, in fact, is the study of rhythm; a beginning should be made in what may be called rhythmical stylistics. The center of attention in this stylistics would be, not the individual complex word or image but the rhythm of individual lines. As in the stylistics of Spitzer, furthermore, the individual unit would not be abstracted from its context, but would be shown at work as part of the poem to which it contributes.

Almost any section of the "Notes" might be chosen as a subject for rhythmical analysis, and I shall isolate the first section of the third part for such an analysis only because, of several sections, it is one which has been consistently misread, as if it is not being heard with the required attentiveness.

> To sing jubilas at exact, accustomed times,
> To be crested and wear the mane of a multitude
> And so, as part, to exult with its great throat,

To speak of joy and to sing of it, borne on
The shoulders of joyous men, to feel the heart
That is the common, the bravest fundament,

This is a facile exercise. Jerome
Begat the tubas and the fire-wind strings,
The golden fingers picking dark-blue air:

For companies of voices moving there,
To find of sound the bleakest ancestor,
To find of light a music issuing

Whereon it falls in more than sensual mode.
But the difficultest rigor is forthwith,
On the image of what we see, to catch from that

Irrational moment its unreasoning,
As when the sun comes rising, when the sea
Clears deeply, when the moon hangs on the wall

Of heaven-haven. These are not things transformed.
Yet we are shaken by them as if they were.
We reason about them with a later reason.
                              (III. i, pp. 398-99)

    The poem is composed of three parts which are integrated
dialectically, both in meaning and rhythm. The first seven
lines present the inferior poetic task of singing in a manner
absolutely at one with the manner of the commonal. If the
multitude is joyous, the folk poet speaks of joy and sings of
it. If the multitude is a giant lion, then the poet is a lion's
head and his tongue is a clapper, tirelessly repeating the
phrases of a single phrase, *ke ke,* a single text, granite monotony. This poet sings monotony monotonously, or chaos
chaotically. He abandons the imagination's Latin and sings
forth the gibberish of the vulgate. The second part, of six
lines, presents the pure poet, not Carl Sandburg but Mal-
larmé, the monastic artist who flees the world and sings only

quintessential, angelic songs. He seeks out the elemental, and, having repudiated the sensual mode, sings those sweeter, unheard melodies. He goes into the desert, stands one-footed on a high pillar, and listens for "The golden fingers picking dark-blue air." The poetry of paganry he eschews; he would hear and speak only the celestial harmony of the spheres. He would be a golden form upon a golden bough. But that form of ethereal poetry satisfies Stevens no more than Yeats. In the third section, of seven lines, he presents the third form of poetry, central poetry, that with which he would ally himself. This is the poetry which compounds "the imagination's Latin with / The lingua franca et jocundissima"; it "tries by a peculiar speech to speak / The peculiar potency of the general." It concentrates on things as we see them, on the things of the world and of the multitude, but it strives to catch the hidden feeling which is as a shadow of that sensual mode of life. This is the "difficultest rigor": to be both lion and angel, common and extraordinary, animalistic and spiritual. Thus, the poetry of the third part of this section is a synthesis of the poetry of the first two parts. It is at one with both and different from either. It is poetry of the real and poetry of the imagined, but it is, really, neither; it is poetry of the real as imagined. It sees things as they really are, not as tranformed, but it sees them as if they were transformed.

The poetry of the first part is, as Stevens says, facile, and its rhythm is free flowing. It is unimpeded, like the roaring of the lion that "roars at the enraging desert." The rhythm of the second part is in sharp contrast to such facility; it is tight-lipped and precise. The rhythm of the third part compounds the other two rhythms; it flows easily but is then, at different points, caught up tightly, interrupting the flow, stalling in a moment of awareness; it is deep breathing interrupted by a catch of breath. Perhaps the surest evidence for the disbeliever is the fact that in the first part there are nine anapests (which enhance the sense of speed and ease), in the second part there is not a single anapest but only iambs, while in the last part (excluding the last line, which is a rider to the whole section) there are five anapests.

More important to the complex rhythm of the poem than these matters of metrics, however, are the variations in syntax. The first part is composed of a series of parallel constructions, each of which moves more swiftly than those before, because of the accumulations of repetitions and the growing certainty that what comes next will be more of the same (to sing . . . to be crested . . . to exult . . . to speak . . . to sing . . . to feel). These forms rise like waves of the gibberish of the vulgate until they fall with the heaviest of feet, the trochee of the seventh line, on Stevens's judgment against such facility: "This is a facile exercise." The syntax of the second part is just the opposite. It begins with a repeated form, three direct objects of the verb "begat" and it includes two "to find's," but it is full of inversions that violate ordinary, idiomatic speech ("of sound the bleakest ancestor . . . of light a music issuing." "For companies of voices moving there, / To find"). Furthermore, this part winds itself up in such intricacies of syntax that it concludes with a form that almost defies analysis ("a music issuing / Whereon it falls in more than sensual mode"). Notice, in passing, how the strict iambic beat forces one to pronounce "issuing" with two strong accents so as to lift the word out of common speech and give it an artificial flavor that it shares with "Begat."

As a synthesis of two other rhythms, the rhythm of the third part is, of course, the most difficult to discuss. The part begins with the most difficult word in the whole section to pronounce, the word "difficultest," which is present to affirm the shift to a third, most complex form of poetry. This part includes its inversions (with "On the image" before not after "to catch," and "its unreasoning" after "from that / Irrational moment," whereas normally it would go before it). But it also includes a parallel sweep like that of the first part ("when the sun . . .

130

when the sea . . . when the moon . . ."). This sweep is more intricate, however, than anything considered so far. The meter is strict iambic, except for a trochee ("hangs on"). But the rhythm works significantly against the meter. Thus, in "As when the sun comes rising," "comes" is the unaccented beat of the foot "comes ris-" and yet it is more heavily accented than the accented beat of the previous foot, "sun." As a result, the voice is truly on the rise when it hits "ris-." As a result of that, it falls off very sharply with "-ing," suggests a pause, a catch of breath, a moment of stillness as one contemplates that routine but extraordinary moment of renewal. The same kind of rhythm determines "when the sea / Clears deeply" with the unaccented "Clears" being heavier than the accented "sea," thus throwing a very heavy accent on "deep" and a peculiarly sharp falling off on "ly." The strain of these conflicts between rhythm and meter thickens and impedes the movement, and conveys the sense of a massive force surging, shouldering its way. Thus the rhythm gives experiential body to a phrase that is close to an oxymoron, since usually we think of deep water as dark or obscure. Finally, in "when the moon hangs on the wall / Of heaven-haven" the word "hangs," functioning as parallel to "comes" and "Clears," but with the added force of a metrical trochee in its support, this word itself hangs at a height, and achieves the climactic pause of the entire section. "Moon" itself is accented; because of "sun" and "sea" we are ready for this accented beat to be followed by another beat with an even heavier accent. Add to that the metrical force and the word coagulates all the force of breathtaking insight that comes to us in central poetry, and we are prepared for "heaven" to be called a "haven." We move, in other words, from "hangs" through a quick fall, "on the," to a moment of repose, but achieved with strong, joyous affirmation (strengthened by three alliterative "h's"). Because of the rhythm, then, we are indeed shaken by these things as if they were transformed.

As for the last line, "We reason about them with a later reason," it stands there, in its wooden flatness, to affirm by contrast that the dialectic just experienced, in all its moments, is nothing like what we might call a rational dialectic. It is that irrational, poetic dialectic, experienced with feeling that is more rational than reason.

Although this section, in all its detail, might now be related to any number of details in the rest of the "Notes," to undertake such connectings would obscure and even violate the point I am making. It is true that this section, in miniature, captures the essential movement of the whole of the "Notes." It brings together and relates, as a *concordia discors*, the major forces of the poem, the non-human world of the sun, the moon, and the sea, with the major abstraction, the idea of man, the commonalty, and with the major man, the poet whose fictions are discoveries, whose imaginings are reality. More important, however, this section brings these forces together with a rhythmical richness of detail that illustrates the true greatness of "Notes toward a Supreme Fiction," a poetic greatness at work throughout the poem, the greatness of that peculiar poetic fusion which unites principle and particle, the cosmic and the minute, in such a way that we experience "the strong exhilaration / Of what we feel from what we think, of thought / Beating in the heart, as if blood newly came, / An elixir, an excitation, a pure power." It is not what Stevens says that is impressive. It is what he says, said as it is said. It is the world as it is, but seen and said by Wallace Stevens, who as poet is himself both the MacCullough and MacCullough.

6

"Esthétique du Mal"

A persistent problem in the criticism of Stevens's poetry has to do with the fact that Stevens insists on the importance of living in a physical world and yet writes poetry, especially in his later poems, that is quite detached from any sense of immediate, physical experience. This apparent contradiction between conviction and achievement must either be explained as significant or condemned as a major failure. This problem is closely related to the clash between those critics who affirm Stevens to be a naturalist, emphasizing man's limited place within nature, and those critics who insist, just as emphatically, that Stevens is an idealist, an advocate of the ultimacy of human thought and imagination and feeling.[1] It can, I think, be solved if considered in the light of this thought of Pascal from his *Pensées,* vi. 348: *Par l'espace, l'universe me comprend et m'engloutit comme un point; par la pensee, je le comprends,* "In space the universe includes and swallows me up like a point; in thought I include it." Man's littleness as a fixed entity within the universe and his magnitude as a thinker about the universe are somehow interdependent.

The force of this paradox dominates one of Stevens's greatest poems, "Esthétique du Mal," but it is already an important aspect of the earlier and simpler poem, "Landscape with Boat."[2] That poem is usually read as a comic satire on nonphysical people, on those who reject the physical, the sensuous, the phenomenal, in order to arrive, by negation, at some ultimate, abstract principle as the truth of truths. If, however, one follows the movement of the poem rather than abstracting an argument from it, he will perceive that Stevens is more sympathetic than not with the "floribund ascetic," with that "Nabob of bones." Stevens takes the ascetic through his process of rejecting the empirical particulars of the world, not accepting any of them because none is the truth, until he arrives at an ultimate which is a mere supposition, a truth that is a mere nothingness. He suggests that the weakness of the ascetic is not so much this upward movement of rejection as the fact of his not carrying the movement to its completion. Having moved so far as to see that nothing is divine (meaning both that no particular is divine in itself and also that the truth itself, the ultimate divinity, is a nullity, a nothingness), by one more step he should have realized that all things are in truth divine. Having seen that transcendent truth is nothing, he should have gone on to recognize that truth can exist only as immanent, is manifested only in its multifarious parts. The climactic image of the poem is the Mediterranean as "emerald / Becoming emeralds." There is an emerald, but it exists only as becoming emeralds. There is what Stevens calls "The rhythm of this celestial pantomime," but it exists only in the tunes hummed by an individual who savors the rich particularity of the scene before him. It is not, then, that Stevens opposes the ascents of metaphysical speculation, the efforts of men to comprehend the universe in thought, but that he finds the true culmination of such ascents to be descents into the physical and sensuous multiplicity of that space which comprehends us. Note, too, that in "Mrs. Alfred Uruguay," the opposite of that ascetic woman who rides up the mountain of abstraction, wiping "away moonlight like mud," is not some rotund sensualist bathing himself in muddy moonlight, is not some imagist or objectivist, but is a "figure of capable imagination" who has been to the top of the mountain and now descends, creating "out of the martyrs' bones, / The ultimate elegance: the imagined land."[3] Only through the artifice of negation can a man realize imaginatively the full richness of the physical world. Only through comprehending the universe in thought, only through a theomorphic adventure in metaphysical abstraction, can one realize the littleness of man as a point in space. Only in being vaster than space can one experience his littleness within it. This is a form of idealism far more naturalistic than traditional naturalism. To posit that objects are really out there, in space, outside one's ego, one must somehow rise above and comprehend both one's ego and the objects outside it. One's humble acceptance of his limitations is dependent upon his proud transcendence of those limitations. What Stevens does, most finely, I think, in "Esthétique du Mal," is to evoke imaginatively this experience of pride and humility, of disinterestedness and interestedness, of man's magnitude and his littleness, of his wealth and poverty, as a single, integral cosmos, as the ultimate "imagined land."

I

There is never a single linguistic context which a critic must accept and use in his efforts to evaluate and characterize any poem. Having experienced the fundamental feeling of a poem as it is articulated by its author, the critic must choose, on the basis of his own knowledge and nature and out of numerous alternatives available to him, that critical language which serves him best in his efforts to capture the unique quality of the poem and to point to it for others to see and to feel. No dogma can absolutely forbid the use of any of the alternatives. The language of a critical school, the language of a particular philosopher, the languages of rhetorical or metrical schemata, biographical, social, or political languages which seem to connect with the poem in relevant ways, the language of other poems contemporaneous or past, the common language itself of the critic, all these may be available to a critic as instruments pertinent, whether in isolation or in combination, to his task of evaluation and characterization.

In viewing "Esthétique du Mal," then, not in the context of other poems by Stevens or in that of certain essays which he wrote about the same time he composed the poem, nor in the context, say, of Santayana's *Dialogues in Limbo,* but in the context of Giacomo Leopardi's poem, "La Ginestra, o il fiore del deserto," I am not suggesting that the other contexts are wrong nor that Stevens wrote his poem straight out of a studious reading of Leopardi's poem.[4] It would not, I might add, be foolish to make this last claim, except that it would imply a derivativeness quite uncharacteristic of Stevens. In truth, the two poems are enough alike to make it quite probable that Stevens knew "La Ginestra"—along with so much else that he uses in his composition of the poem. Both "La Ginestra" and "Esthétique du Mal" are intellectual lyrics, of approximately three hundred and twenty lines, combining argument, exposition, description, and evocative music. Both poems begin in a setting close to Mount Vesuvius, which is smoking and groaning ominously. Both affirm man's helplessness before the ultimate force of nature, a force utterly different from and indifferent to man; and both urge men to join together socially, with compassion and love, in a confederation based upon their inadequacy before the malign force of nature.

The essential similarity between the poems, that which

136

almost commands the linkage I am making, is at an even deeper level. It is that both poems, while insisting upon man's littleness and helplessness, somehow magnify and glorify him. Italian critics are virtually unanimous in their claim that "La Ginestra," though it mocks man's pretentiousness and scoffs at his claims to immortality, exalts the human spirit and encourages men to respect and cherish and assist each other.[5] Though Leopardi views man as no more favored by nature than are ants, though he insists on men's frailty before a natural force like erupting Vesuvius, he affirms the value of human courage in the symbol of the *ginestra,* the yellow flower that covers the black, stony sides of the volcano, a courage to endure pain without cringing or arrogance, a courage not merely to be resigned but to console and assist others, all of whom live under the threat of imminent annihilation. The exultant effect of "La Ginestra" is especially strange, because, as in all his poetry, Leopardi seems quite unself-conscious, quite unaware that he is doing more than belittling man. In order to belittle him, Leopardi ranges throughout the cosmos, imagining man, the earth, even the sun, as no more, taken as a whole, than a point of cloudy light, if viewed, say, from a perspective established on the Milky Way. It is this cosmic range of his own thought that, unawares, exalts one's sense of the human spirit at the very same moment that it is being scoffed at and belittled by the speaking voice of the poet. Thus, the *ginestra* comes to symbolize not simply an innocent, unpretentious being which is to be crushed helplessly by nature; it symbolizes a creature which knows its own limitations and accepts its littleness because of the magnitude of its understanding.

What must be said of "Esthétique du Mal" is that it achieves effects very like those of "La Ginestra," but that it does so with full self-consciousness. Furthermore, Stevens's awareness that man is naught beside Vesuvius but that in his awareness of his nullity he is greater than Vesuvius, this double awareness makes Stevens's poem far more intricate and also far more joyous than Leopardi's poem, which is sufficiently complex and intricate to make it a major achievement of one of the greatest European poets of the nineteenth century.

"Esthétique du Mal" is the study of the beauty of evil, the science of the joyous harmony of man's fundamental faultiness. The poem is an evolvement of Stevens's sense of the beauty of a cosmos in which man's weakness and limitedness is recognized to be an "unalterable necessity." Stevens first evokes a sense of that otherness that surrounds us, a sublime sense of natural force as free of human pain and desire and love. He then develops the feeling of a human society based upon the acceptance of our limitations, a world of "phrases / Compounded of dear relation." He then moves, slowly, carrying us with him so that we share his imaginative experience, into a nonhuman, suprahuman stance from which he views both man's limits and that force which limits him. From this perspective, possible only for a man reclining, eased of desire, in his Mediterranean cloister, Stevens then moves back into the physical world of limited, egocentric perspectives, and rejoices in its richness and multifariousness. He can rejoice in accepting this world only because he has transcended it. Unlike Konstantinov, he is not simply enclosed in his own idea of life, he is not simply limited by his own ego. He accepts that limitedness as a human necessity; but, as a poet who has undertaken the longest meditation, he at the same time views human experience as essentially limited from a transcendental perspective. He concludes the poem not as just another self with its own sensuous world but as an angelic poet, viewing with joy a cosmos composed of

> So many selves, so many sensuous worlds,
> As if the air, the mid-day air, was swarming
> With the metaphysical changes that occur,
> Merely in living as and where we live.

Even in this conclusive joy, however, Stevens is not claiming to be a disembodied angel, a transcendent figure. Even the experience of disinterested meditation, free of desire, has its source for Stevens in bodily desire, in Stevens's own personal form of nostalgia, in his desire to be at home, to be at one with a mother "fierce / In his body, fiercer in his mind, merciless / To accomplish the truth in his intelligence." The split between man as physically limited and man as transcendentally free, the only condition in which the limitedness of man can be recognized, accepted, and appreciated, is healed by the very movement of the poem itself. One experiences his limited position in nature, rejoices in the intimacy of human beings accepting their limitedness; then, with fiercely egocentric striving, moves to a supra-human perspective; and, finally, from that stance free of desire and love and women, moves back in relief to the world of men as limited and partial because of their desires and interests and loves, appreciative of these limitations as only a man who has perceived them as part of a supremacy above them can be.

"La Ginestra" is far more passionate than the "Esthétique." There is something almost ferocious even in Leopardi's keenest and clearest arguments. What is a paradox for Stevens is a genuine contradiction for Leopardi. At no point in his poem does the Italian poet recognize and articulate the oneness in diversity or the concord in discord of man as angelic and man as bestial. Throughout the poem the poet himself is always both angelic and bestial and he is unaware of his duplicity. This peculiar lack of resolution, the tinge of anguish in his joy and exuberance in his misery, gives the poem its ferocity and makes it essentially titanic. Stevens is by no means titanic, nor is there even a moment of dark passion in the whole of the "Esthétique." The poem is rationalistic in the sense that Stevens works out the relation between man as angel and man as beast in such a way as to reconcile and unify them. The union, however, is poetic, not rational. Olympic and serene the poem may be; but even its purest reasoning is impassioned. It is not a philosophical poem; it is an adventure of the mind and carries with it all the feelings, the bitterness and the joy of its quest and of its fulfillment. There is something fearsome in Leopardi's ferocity; but there is something awesome and even uncanny in Stevens too. Leopardi may be something of a lunatic, and Stevens may be a little too sunny for the taste of some. Nonetheless, both poets bring together reason and passion and hammer their feelings and thoughts into superbly complete poems.

II

With this much said, it should now be possible to show how the parts of "Esthétique du Mal" are related without the danger of misleading anyone into thinking of the poem as merely a verbal composition instead of the richly imaginative and realistic experience that it is. The poem begins in this way:

> He was at Naples writing letters home
> And, between his letters, reading paragraphs
> On the sublime. Vesuvius had groaned
> For a month.

The whole of the poem is implicit in these lines. It will be an exploration of the relationship between man as nostalgic, as homesick, as thinking of and longing for home, and man with his sense of the sublime, of otherness, of that which is always beyond him. The man of this first section has his ordinary, bodily concerns, his hunger that lures him out to lunch. But he is also aware that the volcano is outside the range of his experience, that it "trembled in another ether, / As the body trembles at the end of life." The volcano, that is, is alien to his bodily comfort; its nature could be experienced only by one who moved imaginatively beyond life into a condition of death, into a condition free of the will, of desire and feeling.

In this section and in the next, Stevens is suggesting that this deathliness, this unfeelingness, this otherness, of the volcano, of the sky, of nature, of that which rejects us, will save us if we have the courage to recognize and accept it in its essential otherness. At the same time, he sees that it is peculiarly human to shrink from this aspect of the sublime, that the special nature of human pain is to be hallucinatory, that it can hardly endure the sense of otherness as it is in itself. Like Leopardi's *ginestra*, acacias, with their yellow color and heavy scent, are present to remind man of his frailty and mortality and, along with the shadow of night, to point out the otherness of the moon and the sky; they are there to add intelligence to his despair, indeed, to communicate "The intelligence of his despair." The intelligence to which they contribute is that pain is indifferent to the sky, to the painlessness of nature. Out of such awareness, Stevens then, in the third section, criticizes Christianity as the hallucinatory creation of pain. In his pain man hides from his sense of otherness and replaces it with a god "Who by sympathy has made himself a man," who shares our pain with us and cannot be distinguished from us as the truly other, Vesuvius, the moon, the night, and the sky can be. This humanized god is an "uncourageous genesis," created by us out of something akin to self-pity. With the aid of the poet's firm stanzas, which hang like hives with their golden combs in hell, Stevens thinks we ought to be healthy enough to get along without such falsification. As the next section, the fourth, indicates, Stevens associates this humanization of the other with sentimentality, with emotion in excess of its occasion, with pain moving beyond its limits to encompass the sky.

Not, of course, that Stevens opposes transforming the other into the human. Doing that, in fact, is the very task of the true artist, the genius of misfortune. B. at the piano creates a musical world out of a single note, "In an ecstasy of its associates," out of a single sound that is his own, and not out of

141

all sorts of notes that are otherness to him. The Spaniard of the rose rescues the rose from nature by making it exist in his own especial eye. But these representatives of the genius of misfortune know and accept what they are doing. B. knows that his world of music is not the world but his world; the Spaniard knows that his rose is his rose, not "the rose, itself / Hot-hooded and dark-blooded." That is, they accept the basic difference between nature as it is in itself and nature as interpreted, as interpreted by man even in his very perception of it. They accept the elemental faultiness of all human action, the falseness of both our mind and body as they engage themselves with otherness. *Mal,* with all its implications from evil to faultiness and pain and discomfort, is the word to describe everything man does.

Contrary to most criticism of the poem, there is no break at all between the affirmation of the distinction between in-bar and ex-bar and the two following sections, in which Stevens vests the human world with forms that used to be mistaken for the true forms of otherness. Here, that is, terms that were once used to refer to the area of "ex-bar," to otherness, are used in reference to the area of human awareness, the area of "in-bar." In the sixth section Stevens describes human experience as the endless interplay between human creativity, vested in the golden form of the sun, and human doubt and criticism, vested in the form of a big bird with a bony appetite. Human creativity, as the sun, moves again and again to a perfection and then fails, endlessly desiring another consummation. "The sun is the country wherever he is." He is like the single note out of which B. creates his musical world. The big bird of doubt inexorably rejects even the finest human creation, knowing and desiring a further and finer perfection which, in turn, it will reject. In the seventh section, the loveliest of the entire poem, Stevens himself, like the Spaniard, rescues the rose from nature and makes it a symbol of the beauty and value of human sacrifice and suffering, of "the

wounds of all / The soldiers that have fallen, red in blood,"
indeed, of all men, who are soldiers (a metaphor also used
by Leopardi) in the sense that they suffer and die under the
unwavering dominance of natural time. There is nothing easy
or sentimental about this glorification of human death and
suffering. The deathlessness of the soldier of time is a human
creation; there is no pretence that the deathlessness endures in
ex-bar, in the essentially other world. But for Stevens, the uneasiness of the human perpetuation of the beauty and worth
of men who have died is easier than that "deeper death" which
denies that men are wholly human, killing them by the pretence that they are really something other than mortal human
beings.

The eighth section, which begins with "The death of Satan
was a tragedy / For the imagination" is no doubt the most
difficult to experience as an integral part of the whole of the
"Esthétique." Its opening sentence comes so close to being a
commonplace, and the phrase, "the mortal no," has been
abstracted and so distorted from its poetic significance by
critics not concerned with Stevens's poem itself, that the section seems to stand out as a sort of independent tour de force.[6]
Besides, the notion presented here, that Satan ought not to
have been destroyed, conflicts with the idea of the third section, that the health of the world, sweetened by the honey of
the poet's firm stanzas, modifies hell so much that it seems
to have disappeared. How can the earlier approval of the dis-
appearance of hell and Satan be reconciled with this disap-
proval of the death of Satan? Read in the light of what has
already been said in this study, however, the conflict is only
apparent. The hell and Satan that have disappeared with the
approval of the poet are hell and Satan as falsifications of
otherness affirmed as truths. In contrast, the Satan one would
like to have retained is a symbol of human, willful evil,
analogous to the symbols of human creativity and criticism,
the sun and the vulture, and to the symbol of the beauty of

human suffering, the rose that is the soldier's wound. As with the rose, one needs to rescue evil from nature and see it in his own especial eye. Satan, recognized as human fault against nature, as false just because a human symbol of evil, which in itself is quite different from Satanic evil, is as necessary to the imagination as the sun and the big bird and the rose.

The subtlety of this section, however, especially because of the dead weight of our conventional sense of what its phrases mean, involves other difficulties besides this one. Satan has been destroyed. Satan the prince of negation has been negated. This, of course, is a human negation, a mortal no, not a no in nature. "It had nothing of the Julien thundercloud: / The assassin flash and rumble." The symbol of human evil, of the evil inherent in the very fact that each man is by necessity "this unalterable animal," may be negated, but the principle of negation, of human evil itself, can not be negated. This, obviously enough, is so because the very negation of Satan is, as a negation, Satanic. Nonetheless, such a Satanic negation of Satan is a tragedy for the imagination, because it drives evil, fault, and negation underground; it desensitizes men to their elemental faultiness, to all the sons of Satan that lurk invisibly behind every human gesture. These innumerable sons, these phantoms, cannot be destroyed, but they can be neglected. Once we abandon our images of them, along with our image of Satan, they are driven into the silver of "the sheathing of the sight, / As the eye closes." That silver sheathing is a marvelously sharp image of human evil, of the way each man cuts himself off from others, closes them out of his world, whether with contempt or with mere reticence. We all feel this evil as a part of all social intercourse, as a vague uneasiness or embarrassment, but, once we cease to imagine the presence of what we feel, it exists only as a cold vacancy. This very poem, however, though it attempts no revival of Satan, given Stevens's attunement to his age, does revive our sense of the presence of negation, of evil, in the

144

every glance of every human animal. The no to no, the end of one tragedy, is the beginning of another for all who would profit from the poet's imagination. Beneath every mortal no to no lies a passion for yes to no "that had never been broken."

The very existence of the human imagination insures this, as the ninth section manifests. In our epoch of hardheaded common sense in which most of us have lost the folly of the moon, have lost that imaginative lunacy by means of which we rescue objects from nature and humanize them, we all experience the deeper death which is "pure poverty," that sense that nothing human has value, that even our crises are indifferent affairs. We see only what we see and hear only what we hear. This reduction of man to the non-human, to the sub-human, of human speech and sight to mere stimuli and reactions, cannot, however, endure. The very act of human seeing, the human sensibility itself, is a seeing double; there is a seeing and unseeing in the eye. Human speech itself, the phrases "Compounded of dear relation" are "spoken twice, / Once by the lips, once by the services / Of central sense." Once we recognize that the death of paradise is not the death of the paradise of meaning, once we recognize that admitting the fictitious nature of our beliefs does not destroy their reality as fictions, we overcome such destitution. A moment in which the sky is divested of its fountains and all we hear is the chant of indifferent crickets is followed, because we require it as faulty human beings, as imaginative human beings, by "A loud, large water" that "Bubbles up in the night and drowns the crickets' sound." The truth that we require, merely by being human beings, comes to a man just because he is humanly alive. It is "a primitive ecstasy, / Truth's favors sonorously exhibited."

Once these sections are understood, the tenth stanza should come through with clarity and force. It is because of Stevens's elemental bestiality, because his "anima liked its animal / And liked it unsubjugated," that he can recognize how different

145

men are from indifferent crickets, from those "Mechanical beetles never quite warm." He would be at home, he is sick to be at one with his true mother, in the savagest severity, at one with reality as it is. The last nostalgia, for reality explained, reveals that fault itself, that *mal,* that suffering and death are at the innocent heart of human life.

"Life is a bitter aspic." The poet, in section eleven, despises every effort to unify and harmonize human experience and the otherness of nature. But the recognition of the essential painfulness of living, the articulation of these exacerbations, is a pleasure, is the "esthétique" of "mal." People are poor, dishonest, and they die. We are "Natives of poverty, children of malheur." But life, though poor and false and evil, is beautiful because we say it is poor and false and evil: "The gaiety of language is our seigneur."

How can Stevens say such things? He explains, in the twelfth and thirteenth sections, where his nostalgia for "reality explained" leads him. It leads him to escape from both the world of men conscious of each other and from the world of one man conscious of himself into a third world which is pure reality, pure otherness, in which there is no awareness of oneself or of others. To be in that world is to be truly alone. Here, where one is free of the falseness of all fictions, all otherness within oneself or with others, and is at one with otherness itself, the truth of pain is accepted and for a moment there is no pain. This experience of complete oneness with the "force of nature in action," possible only in a Mediterranean cloister where one is "eased of desire," this experience makes him realize that his true love is for falseness and faultiness, for the world of discord and alienation. In such a long meditation, which arrives at the truth that, given the otherness of nature, men cannot but be faulty, destiny is unperplexed as the happiest enemy. "Evil in evil is / Comparative." Nature is essential otherness; being evil is being other, being at fault, at odds, with oneself, with others, with nature itself. Being at odds with nature, with the absolute, is thus, in a deeper sense, being at one with it. Recognizing that nature is absolute evil, that it is "The assassin's scene," one can accept his own assassinations and those of others with a sense of pleasurable harmony. Once one recognizes that the contempt of the "silver in the sheathing of the sight," as his eye closes, is a necessary part of his being "this unalterable animal" within the universal whole, he can cry out, in pain suffused with joy, that the adventure of living is "to be endured / With the politest helplessness. Ay-mi!"

This is reason beyond reason. The rational man, Konstantinov, in section fourteen, is the one who would have all the people "Live, work, suffer and die" within his one logical structure. The suprarational poet, who recognizes that the vastest intellectual structure is not reality but a fiction, is not the ocean but just one more lake, who recognizes how logical system after logical system takes its place in time in its great tomb, this man accepts his place by his lake and permits others to have their places by their lakes. Having been beyond pain, in its utter truthfulness as the inevitable response to that otherness which is the absolute condition of existence, he can now savor pain as the elemental beauty of being a human being. A person unaware of his limits, like Konstantinov, who does not recognize that he is surrounded by other men whose ideas have as good a right to be heard and to be lived as his, this man is a lunatic who cannot distinguish his desire from despair. Seeing, as he does in the last section of the poem, that life is composed of numberless selves, each with its own sensuous world, having been to the rock from which he has observed this elemental faultiness of each self within the universal whole, the poet then affirms the beauty of accepting this tragedy, of living in a physical world. He affirms the wealth and vitality to be found "Merely in living as and where we live." Having gained such wisdom, he would return to live as the lunatic of one idea in a world of lunatics each with his idea. Unlike Konstantinov, he does not strive to impose his idea on others as if they did not have ideas of their own. He would strive to impose his idea fully aware that they will strive to impose their ideas on him. There is no resignation or despair, at least in the ordinary sense of those words, in Stevens's acceptance of his own littleness. Though he accepts the certainty of his failure, like Pascal and Leopardi, he would push his lacustrine principle as hard as he can, he would live savagely and severely. If he would, finally, be indifferent to nature as it is to him, it is only because he has been so attentive to it. That is, he has learned his indifference from it, and from it he has learned that his obligation is to live within the bar, in intimate harmony with all men who, as men, must act out their evil against him as he acts out his against them. Sensing the pleasure and beauty of pain and ugliness does not destroy either pain or ugliness. Once aware that they are unavoidable, one can endure them "with the politest helplessness" and be friends with his enemies, love those he hates, be helpful in his helplessness, and triumphant in his defeat. The very opposite of resignation is what this resignation entails. One lives his ugliness to the full because, having seen its necessity, and having sensed how unbearable inhuman, painless seeing is, he cannot but rejoice in the rich beauty of living as just one more of us "poor, dishonest people."

This is a very different and far more intricate thing than the "radical realism" which several critics have of late attributed to Stevens.[7] Simply to assert that there are real things outside us, unaffected by our ways of viewing them, this is a facile exercise. To ignore the subjective elements in all human thought and perception, to pretend that one can describe objects as they really are, without a taint of personal feeling, as some of our objectivistic poets have tried to do, this is not radical realism, but radical ignorance. A study of their poetry, like Kenneth Burke's fine essay on Marianne Moore in his *A Grammar of Motives,* reveals a latent but dominant personal-

148

ity in even their purest images.[8] Only by acknowledging the unavoidable presence of subjectivity in all human activity and perception and thought, as Stevens does, can one have even a chance of evoking a genuine sense of otherness. Only by evoking that sense, finally, does one have a chance to appreciate the physical world, with all its selves and all its sensuous worlds, "As if the air, the mid-day air, was swarming / With the metaphysical changes that occur, / Merely in living as and where we live."

7

Stevens's Social Poetry

The phrase *social poetry* has several important meanings most of which have no applicability to Stevens's poems. Most often it refers to poetry which presents contemporary men as they are, but viewed in the light of a future ideal that works as a judgment against the present and as a lure to change. Such poetry is activistic, evocative, and often hortatory. Usually notions of this kind assume that men do in fact share an ideal of future life, and that the poet's job is mainly to remind them of this and to prod them into becoming what they truly are. Thus, though activistic, such poetry is also thought of as cognitive, as truthful.[1]

A quite different notion of poetry as social is that which affirms that all great poetry is traditional.[2] According to this notion, true poetry is contemplative and cognitive, not active and evocative. The great poet views man as he is, not as he ought to be and not as he wishes to be. To do this the poet must have a perspective other than some stance adopted by men of action in the present. He may view men in the present from a perspective of eternity, as Dante does in *The Divine Comedy;* or he may view him from the perspective of a past ideal, as Yeats throws the light of the Renaissance ideal of the complete man upon the life about him in "In Memory of Major Robert Gregory," or as Tate in the "Ode to the Confederate Dead" views the modern solipsist in the light of a past community of active heroes; or he may view the present in the light of a myth, the myth of Teiresias or Ulysses or Oedipus or Chiron. Such perspectives, typical of traditionalistic modernism, serve to objectify and to judge man in his present predicament. Without them, a poet, we are told, can but flounder in the vagaries of a wished for future or drown in the waves of the immediate present.

A third notion of social poetry is that the true poem is a focus for the psychic forces of its community; the poem mirrors, objectifies, and concentrates the drives and forces that determine the nature of its milieu. This notion is less restrictive than the first two. The poet is not expected to view the present in the light of the past or of the future, though of course he may do so. His genius determines the way he focuses the drives of his community; his success depends on his doing it, however he does it. A late New Critic, like Frances Fergusson, and a late Communist aesthetician, like Galvano della Volpe, can both accept this notion as superior in its inclusiveness to the futuristic or traditionalistic conceptions of social poetry.[3]

All three of these conceptions of poetry as social emphasize the finitude of man and the mimetic function of poetry, whether for the purpose of luring him to move beyond himself or of judging him as elementally inadequate or simply of portraying him as he actually is. Man as placed in a vision, as fixed in a schematic picture, whether future, past, heavenly, mythic, or immediately present is what one is to attend to in such poetry. A fourth notion of social poetry, which at present is limited mainly to the criticism of fiction, is that of literature as satirical commentary. Men, in black satire, are so small and contemptible that the writer does not bother to show them as they are or to contrast what they are with what they might have been or may become. In fact, in such satirical visions the human figures are so trivial that all value is shifted from them to the satirist himself, to his playful, fanciful acts of mockery and contempt. The pleasure in such satire lies not in truthfulness nor in nostalgia nor in hope but in the very agility of the act of writing itself. Not mimesis but novelty is the key that determines the pleasure of such work.

Except for a few of his early poems, Stevens's poetry is not social in any of these four senses. He is too intensely aware that human reality is to be found not in man as objectified and placed but in man as objectifying and placing, in man as he urgently breaks from feeling into articulation, from desire and intention into action. The human reality and value and vitality of his poems lies not in any character or doctrine or cluster of images fixed and contained within the poems or in their relation to some picture of society provided him by the newspapers or some sociologist or philosopher or theologian for his poetic use. As in black satire, such value lies, always, in the shaping, articulating action of the poem itself. In contrast to the satirists, however, even though Stevens may begin a poem with some figure or some argument to which he is opposed, he is rarely content to leave that figure or argument as something fixed and defined, against which his own thought and imagination and feeling play and rage and develop. He breaks the outer shell of whatever he opposes, senses it inwardly, and makes it live vitally and developmentally along with his own impassioned thinking. He coaxes it into exerting all its living pressure against his own vital sense of reality so that it develops, imaginatively, along with his own imagining. As a result, his poems are often communal dialogues; but no part of the community of his poems is static and fixed; otherness in these poems is as vital and expansive and energetic as the thinking of Stevens's own self. Although his poetry is thoughtful and meditative, it is never contemplative or visionary.[4] What might have been an object within a contemplative vision is invariably transformed into an active, expressive subject whose rights are respected almost as fully as Stevens's own. His poems are overarching actions of thought; but, more important, everything beneath the arch is humanly active too. It is active not as something observed in a detached manner, not as a breathless runner observed coolly from a pavilion; it is active as something in which one participates, even as he continues to carry out his own action. Thus, the extraordinary inwardness of these poems. They are not composed of objects suffused with the feelings and thoughts of the poet as spectator; such objects are themselves turned into active subjects with their own feelings and thoughts and then caught up in the more inclusive action of the poet as thinker and shaper. Not only are the acting subjects within Stevens's poems modified and developed by the overall action of the poem but the action itself is modified and developed in turn by them. Only in this sense can Stevens's poems be called dialectical: not as a dialectical logic but as a living dialectical action. His extreme of illogic is logical. In a quite special sense, his poems may even be called social poetry; they may, in fact, be the only truly social poetry. They are not imitative of a large society composed of small people; they are themselves, as poetic actions, small societies composed of large people.

I

"Reply to Papini," a relatively late poem, is social in this sense, though it contains elements which link it with other forms of social poetry.[5] It contains a figure called Celestin VI, an imagined pope, who views experience from the perspective of heaven, and Giovanni Papini, an Italian contemporary of Stevens, who has advocated that poets should base their poetry on a perspective like that attributed to Celestin. The poem has its element of social activism, for the poet affirms, against Papini, that a poet should not remove himself to eternity but should articulate the movement of men in time, from the present and into the future. A poem, Stevens affirms, is "the growth of the mind / Of the world," which is something like saying that it is a mirroring focus of the psychic forces of its community. The crucial difference, of course, is that for Stevens there is no split between society and the poem; the poem is the society. Finally, the tone of the opening lines

> Poor procurator, why do you ask someone else
> To say what Celestin should say for himself?

sounds satirical, as though Stevens, with mock pity, is going to expose the folly of Papini's notion that poets ought to sing hymns that will console people, hymns of victory even amid the defeats and ruins of the present, hymns like those that popes sing.

These links to other forms of social poetry break apart, however, under the force of Stevens's creative, historical awareness. By the end of the poem the opposition between papal hymns of victory and poetic hymns of "humane triumphals" has virtually disappeared. Both are forms of poetry and both could be hard poetry rather than the easy poetry of the soft sell. Easy poetry is hymns sung amid ruins, of heaven as our already acquired possession. The easy poet would stand in darkness and pain and sing of light and joy as if they were what was real. If there were a Celestin VI—there has been no Celestin since 1296—he might sing such a triumphal. Celestin V did decide that the way through the world was too difficult to find. He was dislodged, losing, that is, his sense of the integral relationship between heaven and earth, and he abdicated. That is why no pope after 1296 has taken the name of Celestin VI.

Hard poetry is "the heroic effort to live expressed / As victory." Out of the formulations of midnight comes the poet as the "angry day-son clanging at its make." His poetry, in fact, is much like a heavenly hymn; it "Increases the aspects of experience, / As in an enchantment, analyzed and fixed / And final." It is not a serene day-son, dissociated in its tranquillity from darkness and pain and death. It has nothing to do with a politics of property, but has all to do with the act of acquiring property, with accumulations going on in the present, with the movement from ruin to victory, from midnight to dawn. So long as papal hymns of heaven were expressive of actual human effort, so long as they were a conception sparkling in the still obstinate thought of actual experience, they were hard poetry too. Now, however, since heaven is a completed acquisition, it cannot be the victory of the heroic effort of men to live in the present. Today the poet, not the pope, is the true heir of those Pope Celestins who lived from the fifth through the thirteenth centuries. Our imaginary Celestin, that is, "Will understand what it is to understand." He will see that the poet today, with his courage to sit in the depths of the world and study silence and himself, "Abiding the reverberations in the vaults," is in truth doing just what popes themselves did during the ages when ideas of heaven were vital outgrowths of the actual experiences of those who conceived them. Thus, it is by his very faith that Giovanni Papini should know how the poet wishes "that all hard poetry were true." Heaven as a gradual accumulation, as an imaginative enchantment that expresses "the heroic effort to live," this is a human triumph. Easy poetry, in contrast, is a triumph which is a defeat; it is not a movement out of darkness and pain into light and joy; it is static, the fanciful expression of a wish for pleasure spoken while one stands helplessly in ruins. Giovanni

Papini, who as an actual man never stood still, who pursued an ideal throughout his career and became an ardent Catholic only after years of independent struggle, he, by his faith, which only gradually became his possession, he too should understand what it is to understand.

What Celestin should say and what the poet should say, each affects and modifies the other. By the end of the poem, earthly poems of victory have their heavenly aspect, and heavenly hymns have their earthly aspect. One's sense of the pope's job and his sense of the poet's job, both have been modified and subtly criticized, each by the other, and both by the movement of the poem itself, a movement fed and clarified by the material it uses, but also a movement which feeds and clarifies that which it uses. The poem as a whole is truly a humane triumphal. Nothing in it, not even the "poor procurator" Papini, is finally repudiated; all is lifted up and activated by the poetic movement of Stevens's thought. This poem excludes the death of objectification, the *rigor mortis* of all visions which fix men and doctrines, delimiting and defining them, so that the poet may achieve a cheap triumph over those he opposes and contemns. No poetry is less photographic than this. The past and the alien, once touched by the vitality of Stevens's imagination, come to life and contribute to the life of his poetry. Otherness is as much a part of the life of Stevens's imaginative self as that self is a part of otherness. Such living capaciousness is far vaster than any panorama which includes objects fixed in space, scattered about on a canvas, and viewed from a single perspective. This poetry is supraspatial as it is supratemporal in the sense that it turns both space and time into the vital human experience of the living present, as the heroic effort to move from the formulations of midnight into the dawn of awareness, like the "angry day-son clanging at its make."

II

It is not difficult to recognize that in "Sunday Morning" Stevens is affirming, in a more sensuous and less dramatic way, something very like the main affirmation of "Reply to Papini."[6] Heavenly hymns or earthly hymns, eternality or life in the immediate present, both, taken in themselves, lack value and beauty and fail to give us contentment, fulfillment, or bliss. Only if our life in time is commingled with and suffused by a sense of timelessness, only if we live our transient lives with a sense of the permanence of death can our lives have value and beauty, only then can we love objects of nature and one another. Pleasure is pain unless integrated with pain. All experience is painful unless one accepts pain as an aspect of all pleasure. That the poem is affirming such things is an easy perception, inescapable unless one becomes embroiled in various doctrinal complications that are of only secondary importance to the poem.

What makes "Sunday Morning" a great poem, however, is that its action, its movement and development, is a living realization of what it affirms. Its every image, its very syntax are charged by the action of the poem and make their contribution to it. Read attentively, the first stanza is full of the movement of the whole poem.

> Complacencies of the peignoir, and late
> Coffee and oranges in a sunny chair,
> And the green freedom of a cockatoo
> Upon a rug mingle to dissipate
> The holy hush of ancient sacrifice.
> She dreams a little, and she feels the dark
> Encroachment of that old catastrophe,
> As a calm darkens among water-lights.
> The pungent oranges and bright, green wings
> Seem things in some procession of the dead,
> Winding across wide water, without sound.

> The day is like wide water, without sound,
> Stilled for the passing of her dreaming feet
> Over the seas, to silent Palestine,
> Dominion of the blood and sepulchre.

It presents two conceptions of life that are equally inadequate: the idea of living one's life for the immediate present, of affirming the value of life in its immediacy, and the idea of living one's life for eternity, for a paradise to be achieved beyond the grave. Reveling in the sensuous pleasures of the moment is as empty an artifice as sacrificing momentary pleasures for the permanence of eternity. Stevens evokes this sense of the interchangeability of hedonism and asceticism and of their equal unsatisfactoriness in every line of the stanza. The inadequacy of immediate indulgence is conveyed by the fact that the mingling of present objects to dissipate "The holy hush of ancient sacrifice" slides directly into its opposite, the holy hush catching up the pleasures of the present and turning them into "things in some procession of the dead." The feeling implicit in "Complacencies of the peignoir," the stasis of such indulgence, is in truth identical with the flat, tedious sense of a world beyond life, which seems like "wide water, without sound." Both, in fact, are dreams, artifices, lacking the spur of actual experience. Consider, for instance, the line so highly praised by Yvor Winters, "As a calm darkens among water-lights."[7] The "calm," of course, has to do with the "holy hush," the religious life of eternity, and it moves into and becomes the "wide water, without sound." But the "water-lights" themselves, catching up and representing sensuous pleasures, the late coffee and oranges and the green freedom of a cockatoo upon a rug, these luminous, flickering lights on the water are quite insubstantial; they are dissipated by the mere dropping of the wind. In turn, the calm that replaces them is truly the same mood as the mood of complacency it replaces. The woman is dreamily sliding from one dream to another and both, in themselves, are equally weightless and ineffectual.

There is a formal sameness to the syntax in which both halves of the experience of this first stanza are presented. The pleasures of the present are given in three similar phrases, each with a noun followed by a prepositional phrase: "Complacencies of the peignoir," "late / Coffee and oranges in a sunny chair," and "the green freedom of a cockatoo / Upon a rug." And the calmness of eternity is offered in three phrases similar to those just quoted: "The holy hush of ancient sacrifice," "the dark / Encroachment of that old catastrophe," and the "Dominion of the blood and sepulchre." Even in its syntax, that is, the stanza presents the two conceptions of life as equally static and artificial and complacent. There is no genuine interaction between the two conceptions; the woman drifts from one to the other with no sense of disruption or transformation, because there is no difference in the basic feelings that determine their natures. A hedonistic Sunday morning is, at bottom, the same as a religious Sunday morning: both rest upon an unbearable complacency and calmness and tranquillity.

In the concluding passage of the poem, the relationship between the present and eternity is entirely different: they are not set off against each other as opposites which are ultimately the same, but instead are integrated as a paradisal earth or an earthly paradise:

> Deer walk upon our mountains, and the quail
> Whistle about us their spontaneous cries;
> Sweet berries ripen in the wilderness;
> And, in the isolation of the sky,
> At evening, casual flocks of pigeons make
> Ambiguous undulations as they sink,
> Downward to darkness, on extended wings.

The fixity of the outspread wings of "the green freedom of a cockatoo / Upon a rug," the artifice of that contrived freedom of the present from the wide water of eternity, has been replaced by the natural descent of the extended wings of the pigeons, which live on our island solitude, "unsponsored, free, / Of that wide water, inescapable." The beauty of the movement of the pigeons lies in the fact that it is not cut off from the wide water, the darkness, which is inescapable, but is integrated with it; this movement occurs in the immediate present but it is suffused with, haunted by, at one with, its very opposite, the sense of the endlessness of darkness, of death, of permanent stasis. The syntax of the passage, too, represents the change that has occurred in the poem. The clauses stand up with their own independence: "Deer walk upon our mountains," "the quail / Whistle about us their spontaneous cries," "Sweet berries ripen in the wilderness"; but each has a natural movement within it in its verbs "walk," "whistle," and "ripen." And, then, instead of being placed next to other clauses of comparable independence, they are followed by the expanding clause of the last four lines, with its tentative hesitations in "in the isolation of the sky" and "at evening" and "Downward to darkness," an expansion, a swirling away from fixity and artificial stasis, in a movement that realizes, tonally, the very essence of the movement that is the poem as a whole.

This final movement of the poem, in contrast to the stasis of its beginning, is bridged by a passage at the very middle of the poem:

> nor cloudy palm
> Remote on heaven's hill, that has endured
> As April's green endured; or will endure
> Like her remembrance of awakened birds,
> Or her desire for June and evening, tipped
> By the consummation of the swallow's wings.

Taken in itself, the passage is truly beautiful. In autumn,

when the swallows are sweeping through the air, gathering for their flight away from "their warm fields," the woman experiences a desire "for June and evening," for the time when she could take for granted the presence of "awakened birds" the next morning. Thus the joy of "June and evening" which she desires and the joy of "April's green" are torn by the poignancy of her sense that what she desires is absent and that the birds in autumn are about to be gone. The fixed spread of the cockatoo's wings upon a rug has been transformed to a true consummation, the spread of the swallow's wings as it reaches the peak of its upward movement. Implicit in this consummation is her recollection of birds that were just beginning to fly, wakened birds, testing "the reality / Of misty fields, by their sweet questionings"; and ominous in this consummation is her sense that it will be followed by the movement at the end of the poem, a movement "Downward to darkness, on extended wings."

Every passage in the poem, for that matter, is pregnant with the sense that one can experience beauty, can love a thing or person, only if he at the same time experiences the painful sense that the loss of that thing or person is imminent, that its mortality is a quality immanent in its living presence. It is Death that

> makes the willow shiver in the sun
> For maidens who were wont to sit and gaze
> Upon the grass, relinquished to their feet.

These maidens had been caught up in the dreamy daze of the immediate present, very like the woman who was taking her "late / Coffee and oranges in a sunny chair." They sat upon the grass, their arms about their knees, gazing at the grass at their feet, relinquished after they had gathered it or simply because they are forgetting it in their dreaminess. The shiver of the willow, willow, willow, however, brings the chill of

161

death into their presence and even the sun turns cold with the imminence of death. Unlike the woman in her sunny chair, they are ripe for love, they will taste not late oranges but new plums and pears offered them by their lovers, and they will "stray impassioned in the littering leaves," loving and lovable because feeling their oneness with "the leaves / Of sure obliteration."

Even the chant of the ring of supple and turbulent men, expressing their boisterous devotion to the sun, is quite different from any primitivism or barbarism based upon a mere acceptance of sensual indulgence as an ultimate good. Their devotion to the sun, unlike the comforts of the sun cherished by the woman in her sunny chair, is dependent on their mutual sense of frailty, on their constant sense that they will perish, on their feeling that their strength is as fragile, as delicate, as transient, as the dew upon their feet. They chant in orgy, it is true; but a part of their chant is the echoing hills "That choir among themselves long afterward." And those choirs of dying echoes establish a oneness between the men with their chant and the pigeons in their descent "Downward to darkness, on extended wings."

Stevens's opposition to Christianity in "Sunday Morning" is as ambiguous as his opposition to the heavenly hymns of the pope in "Reply to Papini." The notion of Jesus and his fellow spirits lingering at the tomb in Palestine, as if it were a porch, beckoning us to abandon our perishing earth and to live for a paradise in which there is no "change of death," this Stevens rejects as he rejects the idea that a poet ought to stand among ruins and sing of heaven as if it were our assured possession. But the sense of Jesus as a commingling of heaven and earth, of Jove and man, as a man who lived and loved the earth utterly because the sense of otherness, of eternity, of death, pulsed through his veins, this figure Stevens accepts almost as a model. He can accept it, to be sure, only by accepting the idea that Jesus, having lived a perishing life, then died. Anything else would be a failure of our blood, which must, like the blood of that god-man, be the blood of paradisal earthiness. If this is a form of paganism—and Stevens does say, in a letter, that the poem is pagan—then one must add that Stevens's paganism takes a highly refined form, a form as dependent upon Christianity as it is upon the paganism that Christianity once routed.[8]

III

Stevens's sense of history is one of the most startling and intricate aspects of his imagining of human experience. This sense is implicit in many of the poems already considered, but in a few poems it is treated quite explicitly. Stevens is aware that we often ignore the pastness of the past and simply make it over, according to our present needs, as a part of the immediate movement of our living present. He is also aware that historians, in contrast to this natural tendency, often respond only to the pastness of the past and cut out of it the vital movingness that is characteristic of our present. Moreover, he is critically aware of the dangers inherent in his distinctions between his own present thinking, of the present as part of his thinking at the moment, and our sense of the present as part of the series past-present-future. Aware that the real present of one's own immediate thinking transcends not only the past and the future as we conceive of them but also the present as we conceive of it, he is also wary of the tendency to fix and degrade the present as a mere picture, as a defined entity, along with the past and future. What he requires of real imagining, of that immediate action of thought, is that, while it distinguishes past from present and the future from the past and present, and all three from its own supratemporal action, it should also be responsive to the reality that unifies them all. To sense the past, the present, and the future, as they really are in the imagination, is to sense in them that living, present movement that they ultimately share with one's own imaginative thinking, which is not so much temporal as creative of time as it functions for human beings.

Much of this intricate sense of history is quite simply expressed in "The Prejudice against the Past."

> Day is the children's friend.
> It is Marianna's Swedish cart.
> It is that and a very big hat.
>
> Confined by what they see,
> Aquiline pedants treat the cart,
> As one of the relics of the heart.
>
> They treat the philosopher's hat,
> Left thoughtlessly behind,
> As one of the relics of the mind . . .
>
> Of day, then, children make
> What aquiline pedants take
> For souvenirs of time, lost time,
>
> Adieux, shapes, images—
> No, not of day, but of themselves,
> Not of perpetual time.
>
> And, therefore, aquiline pedants find
> The philosopher's hat to be part of the mind,
> The Swedish cart to be part of the heart.[9]

Children have no sense of the pastness of the past, but they do have a sense of the livingness of the objects deposited by the past in the present. They, indeed, make these objects over with the feelings and thoughts of their own immediate vitality, they take them in as parts of the immediate action of their minds and hearts. Aquiline pedants, in contrast, scrupulously bar from the objects they study the feelings and vital impulsions of their own present acts of thought. They delimit the objects as things seen, as things whose pastness can be wholly captured in a photograph. For the children the objects are living and present; for the pedants they are past and dead. The poet, as aquiline child, discerns both the livingness and the pastness of the objects, and he laughs jovially at the fact that the pedants cannot see the livingness of the past except as it is experienced as part of the livingness of the present. With more imagination they could retain their sense of the pastness of the past and also sense the livingness of that past as past. There is a prejudice against the past because of both the children and the pedants. The children see it as alive but not with its own vitality; the pedants see it for what it is, but they see it as dead. The children see it as only present, the pedants as only past; whereas the adult poet sees it as the past with the vitality characteristic of the present, as the past made present and the present made past. This is an imaginative version of the idea that all history is contemporary.

The poem is argumentative obviously enough because of its concluding "therefore." But it is, nonetheless, a poem. The lips smack, the tongue clucks, as the poet clips off his lines in mock disbelief that things could go the way they go. The pretence that his own superior insight, synthesizing the truths of both children and pedants and rejecting their falsities, is an obvious thing, that really everyone knows how silly anything short of it is, this marveling assertion of so intricate a sense of the past as though it were a commonplace, makes the poem a joyous and humorous achievement. The poem reminds one of drawings done by Picasso in his old age, done with studied perfection, but as though they were thrown off in a moment, with a few swift strokes.

IV

The major problem for an American poet with a genuine sense of history lies in the fact that American culture is unhistorical. The felt experience available to a poet as an American excludes all those feelings that coagulate about his sense of history. If he would not violate the integrity of his insight into the historical aspect of all human experience, then he would seem to have only two alternatives open to him. He could abandon the peculiarly American qualities of his experience, create an imagined land suffused with traditional elements, and compose poems based upon the experience of a small group of Europeanized Americans. Eliot took this alternative. Or he could view an unhistorical America satirically and critically, from a tradition-laden perspective. This was the path taken by Santayana. Stevens, however, avoids these stale perfections. His imagined land is void of a sense of history; yet it is encircled invisibly, by way of the act of the mind of the poet, by that very sense of history of which it is void. The unhistorical reality is haunted and shadowed by the historical imagining which it denies; and the imagining is realized as that truth, that reality, that is profounder than the reality which denies it. There is no withdrawal, no escape, no evasion from the hard truth that one's reality is unhistorical. Stevens faces and accepts and affirms the emptiness unflinchingly. But he does so with that fuller awareness of the deeper truth which the accepted emptiness excludes and denies. As a result, these poems have the despair of their courage. They are painful, desolate poems. They are so desolate because they contain, as a part of themselves, a sense of what they are not. They are, even so, joyous poems because the poet is aware that the imagined shadow is as real as the desert that denies it. Stevens triumphs in these poems not by escaping into a richly historical world of his own and not by harshly condemning the desolate land from which he will not turn away, but by bringing together the false reality of his land and the true illusion of his own deeper sense of the essentially historical nature of all human experience.

"A Postcard from the Volcano" should be read in the context of these two lines from the later "Esthétique du Mal":

> The volcano trembled in another ether
> As the body trembles at the end of life.[10]

Reclining, eased of desire, the poet becomes the very living of his present thinking; he becomes that present of the movement of thought itself, above the series of the past-present-future and creative of it. From that present, he establishes the future as present, the imagined future of the children as present; and he establishes the actual present of his bodily self as the past of that future imagined as present. What might seem at first a very simple poem is in truth extremely complex as a result of the feelings evoked from the presence in the poem of three actual presents: the present of the thinking poet, trembling as in another ether, supratemporal and supraspatial; the present of the scene on the postcard, the future imagined as present, with its children weaving budded aureoles and picking up bones and saying things about one's mansion and himself; and the present of one's bodily self which is the past of the future as present.

What are the feelings evoked by this temporal complex? Despair, of course, is the most obvious feeling, the despair of one's actual bodily self, of "A spirit storming in blank walls," a spirit sensitive to the fact that its living reality is boxed in the immediate present, with no sense of a rich tradition in its own past and no hope that it will be part of a rich tradition in the future. Its world is a gutted world because it has no future to hope for. Its despair, curiously enough, is produced by its very sureness that children, though they will speak of it and its dwelling with its own speech, will never know that their speech is the speech of him on whom they comment. The quality of objects is determined by the way they are felt and observed by those who live among them. The children observing the mansion of the bodily self of the "I" will see it and speak of it as they do because the "I" saw it and spoke of it as he did. But he saw it and spoke of it as he did be-

167

cause of his certainty that the children, in their innocent un-
awareness of the continuity of history, would treat the past
as if it were not a living part of their present, would treat the
bodily self's present as if it were utterly dead in their present.

Thus, the second obvious feeling of the poem, the children's
innocent wonder as they sit weaving wreaths of flowers and
commenting on the ghostliness of the mansion and its dead
owner, is saturated with its opposite, the guiltiness of their
innocence, of their ignorance that they owe their very eyes
and speech to the dead man, that their vitality is in many ways
a perpetuation of his vitality, which was a despairing vitality
because he was sure in his very bones that they would wonder
about him with their ignorant innocence of history and its
efficacy.

The dominant feeling of the poem, that of the living present of the poet's immediate thinking, may be summed up in
the phrase, "The gaiety of language." The poet shares the
despair, the aching desolation, of his bodily self but, as experienced by this man as poet, the despair becomes "a literate despair" that cries out in all three presents, but mainly in
the supratemporal present, as above and "Beyond our gate
and the windy sky." From that other ether, the poet experiences the jubilance of knowing the intricate relationships
between past and present and future within the time series.
As a result of such knowing, the whole of the world of the
poem, the dirty mansion, the children, the bones left behind,
the way things are seen and felt, and speech itself are all
"Smeared with the gold of the opulent sun," with that supratemporal source of light and awareness that is the very moving
of the poet's thought in the present of this poem as a living,
imaginative experience. The despair of what will become
mere bones to be picked up by children, the guilty innocence
of the children, these remain the anguish and the ignorance
of this desolate world. While the words continue to tremble
and echo from the volcano, however, while this supratemporal

linguistic awareness continues to smear the dirt and poverty of the scene with the gold of its opulence, the despair felt cries out as "a literate despair" and "The gaiety of language is our seignior." The gold is merely smeared on the dirt; the dirt remains what it is, covered by the gold, but as real as if exposed. Despair, guilt, ignorant wonder, jubilance, and gaiety, all survive and contribute vitally to this richly historical and desolately unhistorical affirmation of an imaginative truth.

V

"Dutch Graves in Bucks County" is the fullest realization of Stevens's sense of the historical continuity underlying the unhistorical quality of American experience.[11] In this poem, there is an unbridgeable gap separating Americans in the present, fighting World War II, and their Dutch forefathers, who originated our civilization in the seventeenth century. The feeling of this gap persists throughout the poem. It is apparent in every one of the twelve stanzas of the poem, each of which is divided into five lines devoted to the present and two lines directed to our Dutch ancestors, who are now in their graves. But our sense of this gap is countered, with increasing force as the poem develops, by an opposite feeling, by our sense that there is a fundamental identity between the present and its origin in the past. The very basis of the life of our Dutch forefathers was their conviction that they must break with their past, tearing up all the inheritances normally descending to them, and must experience their own ecstasy as the glory of heaven in the wilderness of America, as a utopian realization of the New Jerusalem in this new-found land. Their sense of the need to diverge from the past, furthermore, is the very basis of our sense that we must diverge from them. The need to diverge, to experience one's own freedom in one's own way, is thus recognized as a traditional need; discontinuous experience, from generation to generation, is the underlying continuity that binds us to those we reject. Our freedom from the past has its origin and basis in the past. Living within the present, realizing fulfillment not in the past or in the future, this untraditional sense of life is a traditional way of life that had its inception in those who "in the total / Of remembrance share nothing of ourselves."

It is obvious that this paradox of our being bound traditionally to those from whom we are free is the underlying conception of "Dutch Graves in Bucks County." It is not so obvious, however, that the paradox is fully though subtly present even from the beginning of the poem and in each of its following stanzas.

> Angry men and furious machines
> Swarm from the little blue of the horizon
> To the great blue of the middle height.
> Men scatter throughout clouds.
> The wheels are too large for any noise.
>
> And you, my semblables, in sooty residence
> Tap skeleton drums inaudibly.

The first thing that strikes one in this opening stanza is the utter difference between present experience and our Dutch ancestors. We swarm and scatter, freely and magnificently, through the sky, whereas our ancestors, forever earth-bound, are gathered, in their tininess, in the earth. The continuity between us and them is already implicit, however, in these first lines. Our movement is "from the little blue of the horizon / To the great blue of the middle height." Our origin was a little point, a fine, hardly discernible point, it was no doubt in the special quality of the life of our Dutch ancestors. The words "swarm" and "scatter" counter the sense of our grandness and associate us with flies or insects, buzzing all over the sky, not entirely different from the tiny, sooty Dutch soldiers who are now in their graves. Furthermore, though our wheels are so large and the drums of the Dutch so small, both are beyond hearing: the one is too large for any noise, the other too small. The present, in the immediacy of its movement, is simply beyond containment, even by the ear; the past, in its remoteness, cannot be caught and thus contained by the ear. The remoteness resulting from vastness and the remoteness resulting from smallness thus draw together, as an identity, the apparently so different past and present. Even in this first stanza, then, the phrase "my semblables" is not merely ironic. Those who seem so different in their remoteness from us are, at a deeper level, the true semblables of present Americans. There is an unreality in the expansiveness of the present not so very different from the unreality of those "skeleton drums" being tapped inaudibly in the graves of our ancestors. In the hearing of the imagination, however, both are more real than the sounds our physical ears can contain.

Moreover, the quality of the last two lines of the first stanza, concentrated only on the past, permeates the first five lines of the second stanza, which are ostensibly directed only to the present, to the vast masses of men moving and marching together as part of modern warfare. These violent marchers of the present are said to be "shuffling on foot in air," "shuffling lightly, with the heavy lightness / Of those that are marching, many together." The tonal quality of this passage is tightly bound to that of the passage in which our ancestors "Tap skeleton drums inaudibly." The massive movements of the present are marching to a rhythm being beaten inaudibly out of the past.

The underlying oneness of vastness and tiny remoteness as both uncontainable is one of the dominant motifs of the poem, linking the past and the present together as identical. Another motif, which becomes increasingly important in the progress of the poem, is the sense in the present that it will be incorrigibly cut off from its future when that future is the present, just as the Dutch ancestors are now cut off from the actual present.

> This is the pit of torment that placid end
> Should be illusion, that the mobs of birth
> Avoid our stale perfections, seeking out
> Their own, waiting until we go
> To picnic in the ruins that we leave.
>
> So that the stars, my semblables, chimeres,
> Shine on the very living of those alive.

The joy that comes with the effort of fully realizing one's heavenly ecstasy in the present, of achieving a perfection of one's own, is qualified by the sense that just such a commitment assures that one will be rejected and abandoned by those "mobs of birth" that are to follow. The pathos attending this, at first felt as appropriate only to one's tiny ancestors, now comes to be a feeling relevant to one's own present experience. The opening notion that movement in the present is from the little blue of the horizon to the great blue of the middle height, from the small to the vast, is now seen to reverse itself and to go back toward the horizon, now not a place of origin but a place of termination. The rumbling of the violent marchers of the present occurs "along the autumnal horizon." Because the creative independence of each new American generation depends upon its killing off its fathers, its very act of freedom is suffused with the pathetic sense that it too will be murdered as part of the creative acts of those who follow it.

> Time was not wasted in your subtle temples.
> No: nor divergence made too steep to follow down.

These concluding lines of the poem make unmistakably clear the fact that this poem, though seeming only to affirm the discontinuity of American experience, is also affirming the continuity of this discontinuity. Time was not wasted. Our Dutch ancestors, in their time, created a sense of time, of time as discontinuous from generation to generation, that is still our sense of time. Their temples were subtle in the sense that they were small and thin and remote, but also in the sense that their religion of freedom, which seems to be the basis of our freedom, is also the basis of our servitude. That is, there was something insidious in the power of their break with tradition: it established a tradition of breaking with tradition, and this tradition, it would seem, is one which we cannot escape, one to which we are irrevocably bound. Our freest act, even an effort to break with the very tradition of breaking with tradition, would simply be another divergence, another variation of the pattern established long ago, another confirmation of its inexorable power. Thus, those pitiable Dutch ancestors, who seemed so little, locked in the smallness of their rejected past, become, at the end of the poem, awesomely powerful and omnipresent. Divergence was not made too steep to follow down. But there is nothing to do but "follow down," down the autumnal horizon to sure annihilation. One accepts the inevitability of his freedom, but recognizing that it is a form of servitude, accepting it as a part of the "action of incorrigible tragedy." The poem is a poem of piety: it exalts one's pitiable forefathers and affirms one's allegiance to them. But there is no abandonment of the present in Stevens's piety. It is a furious and an angry piety. His very awareness of the servitude inherent in his freedom makes the historical sense of the poem original, profound, and modern. It takes a vast mind to recognize the littleness of oneself not only in space but in time. The mind recognizing this is much vaster than all those human forces swarming, free of care and expansively, throughout space, oblivious to the chains binding them to those they have rejected and from whom they feel themselves to be free. With no touch of sentimentality or nostalgia, with the sheerest austerity, Stevens has resurrected those ancestors we have killed. No poet hereafter, even if as fine as Robert Lowell, can abandon his tradition of no traditions with a complacent sense of sure success. "Fate is the present desperado." Because of poems like this, however, one can turn his despair into a "literate despair" and achieve a freedom of insight and awareness that goes beyond the servitude of his freedom.

8

The Commonplaces of Old Age

American poets have not, in general, aged well, because they have been unwilling to live their agedness with any fullness of being. If one's bodily vigor declines, then it seems that the subjective thrust of his imagination must be blunted too. There is an assumption current in our culture that the human subject is no other than the human psyche, and, since the psyche is intimately at one with the body, a decline of the body entails a decline not only of the psyche but also of all the forces of the human subject, the imagination included. In his old age, the American poet becomes the good gray poet, not the green poet of the goodness and grayness of bodily decline. Stevens has written his poems of old age against just such a background of commonplaces. His late poems are not the withered poems of old age, nor are they a raging against the withering away of the body. They are rather the vitally imaginative realizations of the elemental qualities of the withering process of the body at the end of life. They are not

175

aged poems, but they are based upon an acceptance of the aging of the body. Their distinctiveness is, of course, a limitation; they cannot serve as models to be imitated by youthful poets. Just as emphatically, however, they are not defective as poems because of the agedness contained within them; and thus it is unjustifiable to claim that they are not poems so much as amateur philosophy or something which trancends our idea of the nature of what poems are or can be.[1] When they work, these poems are genuine poems which articulate the intimate qualities of certain experiences which are not, or not yet, directly available to most readers.

These poems are strange and difficult, and should seem so to most of us, just because nothing in our tradition, not even Stevens's own earlier poems, has prepared us to respond to them sensitively. Their difficulty does not lie in their private or solipsistic nature, as Joseph Riddel has suggested. For longevity is a public fact of our culture. The poems may, of course, seem private and solipsistic to a reader who does not overcome the taboo against attending seriously to the intimate feelings of the aged. It is also true that unarticulated feelings do not truly exist, so that, until Stevens wrote these poems, feelings associated with old age have had such crude public expression that a sensitive critic, young or old, would have been foolish to take them seriously. All this changes, however, with the creation of these poems, which are the full expression of the most intricate qualities of old age, qualities so strange that they seem as remote as words from paradise.

Not the withering of the body, the dulling of one's hearing, and the blurring of one's sight, not these aspects of the poems make them difficult to read. We know enough about such things, carrying them in our bones as our future; in fact, that is why we turn away from the aged and concentrate upon youthfulness. The difficulty of the poems lies rather in the savage and joyous imaginative awareness with which Stevens observes and expresses these processes of withering and dulling and blunting. We could be at ease with the poems if they were simply asserting an absence of the imagination as characteristic of old age, of the autumnal period of life. What astonishes us and provokes our awe is Stevens's ferocious imagining of that very absence of imagination. To be "Inanimate in an inert savoir" is one thing. To be imaginatively aware of oneself as "Inanimate in an inert savoir" is quite another. The very difficulty of mouthing such a line, as one must in that strangely appalling poem, "The Plain Sense of Things," is the kind of difficulty which these poems force upon us.[2] Following the sad efforts of an old man trying to choose the adjective for "this blank cold, this sadness without change" is quite different from following the vital imagination of a poet who is aware of this difficulty and who moves swiftly and courageously in his articulation of such dull inertness. There is a harshness and cruelty in such withering into truth from which we avert our soft, indulgent, youthful eyes and ears. We hold back, fearful before such ruin and poverty, and thus miss "the afflatus of ruin," the "Profound poetry of the poor and of the dead."[3] Only if we can endure the starkness of

> The great pond,
> The plain sense of it, without reflections, leaves,
> Mud, water like dirty glass, expressing silence

> Of a sort, silence of a rat come out to see

only if we can enter into the feel of that "Water like dirty glass" and the "silence of a rat come out to see," can we go beyond it to share Stevens's paradisal vision in which "eyes open and fix on us in every sky," that "visibility of thought, / In which hundreds of eyes, in one mind, see at once."[4] It is with the eyes of old age that "you look / At the legend of the maroon and olive forest"; but seeing those old eyes seeing, as Stevens does in "The Green Plant," is to see with an inner, imaginative eye, a supraseasonal eye; it is to be that green plant that "Glares, outside of the legend, with the barbarous green / Of that harsh reality of which it is part."[5] It is to experience a fresh spiritual, "A coldness in a long, too-constant warmth." It is to experience a "polar green, / The color of ice and fire and solitude," a home beyond our every sense of home, an innocence the tenderest part of which is the imminence of disaster.

There is an oddity of perspective in these poems that wrenches our eyes more violently than the most difficult of abstract paintings. There is an eye of eyes, an ear of ears, a voice of voices and, if the reader had not entered into old age, they would have seemed to be mere Platonic ideas, non-experiential abstractions, phantoms not to be countenanced by those whose thought must always be faithful to life itself.[6] But what would have seemed bodiless and formless to the body and form of youth and middle age turns out to be the very form and body of old age. It is bodiless only for the body's slough, only for the forms one abandons as he moves into the strangeness of his antiquity. This strange agedness is, fundamentally, a seeing double, a sensing in which "Real and unreal are two in one," the sensing of a man who turns blankly on the sand somehow at one with the sensing of the aurora borealis, of "eyes that open and fix on us in every sky." In this state

> The enigmatical
> Beauty of each beautiful enigma
>
> Becomes amassed in a total double-thing.
> We do not know what is real and what is not.[7]

It is a bringing together of the distant and the near, of this illumined large and the veritable small; it is as mysterious as two parallels becoming one, "a perspective, of which / Men are part both in the inch and in the mile."[8]

In the best of his earlier poems Stevens struggled to unite

and harmonize his animal self and the fictive force, MacCullough and the MacCullough, and the struggle itself was the
propelling force of the poems. Because of the struggle, the
reader could work his way into the experience of this *concordia discors* which was beyond his own egocentric nature
but not utterly distinct from it. In these late poems, however,
there is an ease of mind that begins and ends with a oneness
of twoness; all the struggle and violence of yoking disparate
elements together has been superseded. This lack of difficulty
within the poems is, in fact, the major obstacle to an appreci-
ation of the poems. One asks if Stevens has not lost his hold
on the complexity and intricacy of experience and if he has
not abandoned serious poetry for fanciful daydreaming. The
answer lies, I think, in the recognition of the fact that the
body of the aged man has lost its vigorous efficacy, its power
of reaching outward and grappling objects to its animal
bosom; it has lost its expansiveness, its resiliency, and has
become a rigid object, unlighted from within. As a balance
to this shivering residue of a man, the poet's imagination has
flowed freely beyond its body and become one with the power
of the supra-egoistic imagination. There is still a twoness in
the even flow of the poems, but the turbulence of opposition
has passed away. The ease of mind which dominates these
poems does, then, exclude the tenseness and opposition of
other forms of experience, but it is not, for that, non-experiential. It is faithful to life, as Stevens's imagination has always
been, but the life to which it is faithful is the life of old age.

I

My first reaction to the climactic lines

> Within its vital boundary, in the mind,
> We say God and the imagination are one . . .
> How high that highest candle lights the dark.

of the "Final Soliloquy of the Interior Paramour" is that Stevens has simply not earned them.[9] The whole poem seems too easy. It begins:

> Light the first light of evening, as in a room
> In which we rest and, for small reason, think
> The world imagined is the ultimate good.

The paramour interior to the man is at the same time interior to the whole world. Would this not suggest that there should be a certain resistance in the poem? The innermost lover of the whole world must surely appear to be exterior to the man in his room. The experience of age, however, denies the resistance. The candle in the room is the evening star; the room is the world; the imagination is God; a dwelling is the evening air. The paramour is a "we," both small and large, but the difference between man and God is forgotten and everything that makes of "we" "each other's" evaporates as man and muse become one with the obscurity of an order, a whole. This is a special comfort of old age: the ability to forget the bodily rigidity of one's self and to melt into the air and become one with the force that inspires it. Such an ease of mind is not the culmination of an effort to integrate opposites; it is an exclusive ease in which man and muse collect themselves by turning away from all the indifferences, all the things that cannot be integrated into this intense rendezvous. The poet-muse knows they are poor, knows that their oneness is exclusive; thus, in a way, the dark, recalcitrant things that have been excluded are a part of the poem as excluded. The sense of the fancifulness, of the unreality, of the oneness of the experience keeps the poem from being fanciful and unreal. Even so, the excluded things are not felt as an ominous threat; the poem is dominated by the dreamy pleasure of neglecting the othernesses of the world and of one's own body. The poem must seem silly unless it is taken as a delicate articulation of the comfort experienced by an old man whose imagination has escaped from the tentacles of his body and flowed into a oneness with what he feels to be the governing force of his world.

The same easiness dominates "The River of Rivers in Connecticut" so that its flow is in marked contrast to Stevens's earlier, more flashy and disrupted poems of movement like "Domination of Black."[10] Unlike the vital, integrative movement of that early poem, the river of rivers in this poem is neatly abstracted from any sense of death. Stevens is quite deliberate here; he affirms the river, the forceful flow that underlies the appearances of the world and is yet the very movement of his own mind as an abstraction far this side of Stygia. And he celebrates this river and the gaiety of its mere flowing as a movement that excludes all sense of Stygia, the first black cataracts, and trees that lack the intelligence of trees (that is, trees of death, trees not composed of and at one with the intelligence of men who observe them and think of them). How can such a seemingly arbitrary abstraction be genuinely and experientially poetic? It is not, I would insist, any phenomenological cut, any *epoché*, which permits the poet to analyze the intentional object with ease. It is rather a crucial aspect of Stevens's sense of agedness. A sense of death, curious as it may be, is immanent only in the life of one whose mortal body is vigorous. When the force of the mortal body wanes, the fear of death dissolves. There is a suggestion in the poem that the forceful flow of old age, unclogged and unrestricted by animal vitality and thus free of the horror of death, is itself strikingly similar to the river of death. Be that as it may, or even if because of that very similarity, the poet delights in the flow of his imagination, "Flashing and flashing in the sun," without a touch of anxiety over the imminence of death. The consolations of age are not slight.

Because of the gaiety of the unnamed flowing of the poem and its trees and steeple, one might wish to burke it and suggest that it is related to the prodigious flow of urine that old men are continually abstracting from their systems.[11] The sentence "The steeple at Farmington / Stands glistening and Haddam shines and sways" would be a good place to start on such a venture. But there is a lack of the scatological in Stevens, even as an old man, so that such an effort would be illicitly fanciful. No doubt the pleasure of not damming up one's urine very long and of constantly letting go resembles the feeling of gaiety in the poem. The poem, however, does not profit by way of such an appendage, which is not organic to its body.

A question sure to be asked at this point is whether this easy flow of the imagination of an old man and its identity with the flow of the world and the force of the fictive muse can be reconciled with those late poems in which Stevens, more unequivocally than ever before, affirms the reality of an object in itself, an object beyond the mind. If the imagination does flow beyond the old man's body and psyche and commingle with the objects of the world, does this not directly contradict the possibility of there being objects outside the mind? At least in Stevens's sense of things, which is always experiential rather than philosophic, it does not. After all, the object in itself, the scrawny cry of "Not Ideas about the Thing but the Thing Itself," the leaves that cry in "The Course of a Particular," and the gold feathered bird in "Of Mere Being," these things that are said to be outside the mind are given whatever reality and being they have within the imaginative affirmation of the poem itself. That eerie vision, "The bird's fire-fangled feathers dangle down," is undeniably created by the imaginative words of the poet; the words contain the bird within them, they do not point to some existent creature outside them.[12] This is poetry of old age, not of senility, and Stevens knows what he is doing.

As the body in old age shrivels and withdraws into itself, the objects around it curl away and separate from it. The old man of "The Course of a Particular" may say that he is a part of everything, but "being part is an exertion that declines."[13] "Today the leaves cry." The old man can have no bodily feeling for and no oneness with leaves that cry. Leaves simply do not cry, by any stretch of the human imagination. That these leaves cry pushes them away from us; we cannot be responsive to so farfetched a suggestion. Thus they are indeed "the thing / Itself" and their cry "concerns no one at all." The leaves do not transcend themselves; there is no "fantasía" to connect the leaves with the old man, to evoke a response, a feeling that relates them. Does this not involve Stevens in a contradiction? He, after all, is responsive as poet to the leaves as things that cannot evoke a response and to their cry as a cry that concerns no one at all. But that is the crux of all these poems of old age. Once the body has withdrawn into itself, the imagination moves beyond it to become one with the world that is separate from that body. It is a cold imagination by means of which even the absence of the imagination, of fantasía, is imagined. To affirm a body and a cry as separate from each other, as outside each other, one must imaginatively transcend them both and contain them within the suprabodily movement of one's imagination. The leaves cannot honestly be found to be things in themselves by means of the human body; but they can be found to be such by the disembodied imagination which has become one with the air and weather of the world. The imagination of these late poems, then, is in one sense a nonhuman imagination, though, as an aspect of human old age, it has a humanity that goes beyond our ordinary notion of humanity. It is an incorporeal body, still human, "Another bodiless for the body's slough."

If the poem is read in this way, then the word "air" in the next-to-the-last line of the version now preserved in the first printing of the *Opus Posthumous* is preferable to the word "ear," which appears in the Spring, 1951, issue of *The Hudson Review* and in the second printing of the *Opus Posthumous:*

The leaves cry. It is not a cry of divine attention,
Nor the smoke-drift of puffed-out heroes, nor human cry.
It is the cry of leaves that do not transcend themselves,

In the absence of fantasía, without meaning more
Than they are in the final finding of the air, in the thing
Itself, until, at last, the cry concerns no one at all.[14]

"Air" is superior to "ear" because even the final finding of
the ear could not be that the leaves do not transcend themselves. The ear is, after all, bodily and affects everything it
hears merely by hearing it. If "ear" is insisted upon, then the
ear must be an ear of ears, a grotesque, elephantine ear. In contrast, the final finding of the air, of the air with which the poet's
disembodied imagination has been identified, could be just
that: that the leaves are themselves and nothing else. The cry
of the leaves does concern the liberated imagination as a cry
that concerns no one at all. For that imagination, disembodied, at one with the world, detached from animal heat, truly
disinterested, is in fact no one at all; it is more like hundreds
of eyes that open and fix on us in every sky. All of which
suggests that one should not deny the possibility of disinterestedness and detachment until he has entered into the period
of his old age. No, the positing of an object in itself, outside
the mind, does not conflict with the oddity and easiness that
are characteristic of these poems; without clash or strain,
these things are perfectly at one.

II

If the reader associates these last poems with phenomenology, the proper way to take this is to say that a certain agedness works at the roots of phenomenology, not that that philosophical position is the basis of these poems. Philosophy as
doctrine has no more to do with these poems as poems than
it does with Stevens's earlier achievements. Even the superb
"To an Old Philosopher in Rome" must be read not as doc-

trine but as aged experience.[15] The poem is not to be distinguished by all the sets of opposites that it brings together: the majesty of the movement of men with their increasing smallness, Rome as the city of God with Rome as the city of men, the celestial possible with the light of a candle, being full of pity and being pitiable, commiserating and being miserable, afflatus and ruin, the blood of an empire and a last drop of blood from the heart of a man, paradisal speech and poverty, and the immensest theater and a book and candle. The poem is to be distinguished rather by the utter oneness of all these opposites in the immediate experience of a dying man. The dying man is "commiserable." He shares the misery of the veritable smallness of all of us; his dying body is as inert and insignificant as his pillow. As observed from the outside, intent on his "particles of nether-do," he is absurdly pathetic. But in utter oneness with this miserableness, he is a man of commiseration, a man of sorrows, a man whose vision has grandeur and afflatus, a man whose very experience of poverty creates in him a sense of heavenly mercy, just as his mercifulness sharpens, even creates, his sense of impoverishment.

That the identity of Rome as earthly and Rome as celestial is experiential rather than theoretical is suggested near the very beginning of the poem. The identity occurs "in the make of the mind":

> It is as if in a human dignity
> Two parallels become one, a perspective, of which
> Men are part both in the inch and in the mile.
>
> How easily the blown banners change to wings . . .
> Things dark on the horizons of perception,
> Become accompaniments of fortune, but
> Of the fortune of the spirit, beyond the eye
> Not of its sphere, and yet not far beyond

One is required to imagine the earthy Rome as one parallel,

with its figures in the street, its blown banners, and its dark things, its newsboys, domes, and bells; and to imagine celestial Rome as another parallel, with its wings, its murmuring and fragrance as part of the total grandeur of its total edifice. Then one must slide the parallels into one so that they are identical. Parallels, of course, cannot even touch, let alone occupy the same place. But that is just the miracle of old age on the verge of death that is the basis of the whole poem. The miracle occurs wholly within the intimacy of the room where the old philosopher lies dying. In the dimness of his dozing in that room, a dimness which blurs his perception of his bed and books and chair, of the nuns attending him and the candle, he experiences an otherworldly wakefulness, in which there is

> a portent
> On the chair, a moving transparence on the nuns,
> A light on the candle tearing against the wick
> To join a hovering excellence, to escape
> From fire and be part only of that of which
>
> Fire is the symbol: the celestial possible.

In the intimacy of a dozing-wakefulness, that is, he experiences a perfect reconciliation of the actual and the possible, of poverty and afflatus, of the architecture and bells of Rome and the silence and solitude and mystery of a celestial perfection. And all this occurs with the utmost ease and serenity, as if the dying man simply spoke words concerning so total a grandeur and then, in the very speaking, the grandeur was realized. Or, since the words of an old man dying are inaudible, since the very words of the man of this poem partake of the identity of actuality and possibility, the whole miracle occurs in words so muffled that they do not quite reach the level of speech. The poem itself is identical with the bliss that death brings to the thinking man.

> He stops upon this threshold,
> As if the design of all his words takes form
> And frame from thinking and is realized.

For all the vast and phantasmal identifications going on in the poem, it is by no means a facile exercise. The difficult task of the poet is to remain faithful to the imagined experience of the dying man, in his dreaming-thinking-speaking-feeling grandeur and weakness. The poem is monotonal, one must grant, in the sense that the things brought together within it are fully at one from the start. The triumph of the poem is a thinness, a calculated vagueness and unresolvable ambiguousness, a oneness that defies our deep sureness that things so disparate must be integrated, not serenely identified. In its fidelity to the life of the most commonplace of all experiences, the actual experience of a man dying, the poem violates every canon of modern poetics. In its faithfulness to experience, the poem is irrefutable proof that Stevens's final loyalty was never to abstract principles, to the manifesto of any poetic movement, to any structure of philosophy, even to any complex of philosophical problems. The actual, vital movement of the poet's shaping, in the present, as it is and not as it was, is the absolute that makes Stevens's best poems the supreme achievement of modern American poetry.

III

All the feelings worked out in one or another of the poems of this period are strained to their highest pitch in what is, I believe, the greatest of Stevens's last poems, "The Auroras of Autumn."[16] The progress of the poem is the breaking down of all forms, all containers, all houses, cabins, homes, theaters, all shapes within which a man may have a sense of place and an ease of possession. And yet as house gives way to house and festival to festival, it is gradually realized that in the freest

imagination there is an uncontainable container, an unhous-
able house, a home that is unlike any home, a "hall harridan"
in which the unhappiness of men and the happiness of the
world are utterly at one, "Like a blaze of summer's straw, in
winter's nick." The image for this supreme oneness is the
auroras of autumn; as a human quality, it is that finally
achieved innocence, an innocence that is essentially the imminence of disaster.

In no other long poem does Stevens achieve unity by means
of a single, recurrent image, as he does here with the auroras
of autumn. Stevens's sense of the ultimacy of movement, of
ever-changingness, precluded his use of a single, delimited
image to contain the imaginative movement of a poem. In the
auroras, however, he discovered an image that lacked the
delimited characteristic of imagery. The auroras are an image
that is really not an image. They are lights that flash and fade
in their very flashing. They rise luminously out of darkness
and sink back into it all in the same moment. They blaze as
an essential part of darkness. They flare with the brilliance
of an active, aggressive father, yet they sink back into a soft,
motherly darkness. It is, of course, the utter oneness of light
and dark, of father and mother, of being and death, that
makes them so harrowingly joyous a realization of the imagination. Taken in themselves, they would be unbearable; the
father's action would be frigid and the mother's darkness
mere annihilation. As unified in the imagination, however,
as the oneness of dawn and evening, of auroras and autumn,
of birth and death, they realize the most ecstatic, mystical,
paradisal, disastrous innocence to be found in the poetry of
Stevens.

Most criticism of "The Auroras of Autumn" breaks down
under the critic's failure to identify and delimit the meaning
and significance of the images within the poem. This unfixedness of imagery is, in truth, a difficulty which faces many
critics in almost all of Stevens's poems. Stevens was never so

stolid a carver as, say, to identify green with reality and blue with the imagination, and then to use the colors as consistent symbols thereafter. In this poem, however, the unfixedness of the images truly reaches an extremity. Within the context of the image-nonimage, action-nonaction of the auroras, every other image flashes and fades as it flashes into something else. By the end of the poem, for example, one is quite sure that the serpent of the first section is a symbol of time, of metamorphosis, of evil, of wisdom, of the verbal imagination, with its "expressive tongue," its "finding fang," and of all of life and reality themselves. Even as it is presented in the first section, however, the serpent is evidently and mainly the auroras of autumn; it seems to be "form gulping after formlessness" which is immediately recognized to be another "form gulping after formlessness." The lights flash and fade into a darkness which immediately becomes another form of lights fading into dark formlessness. As one watches the serpentine lights of this section, he anticipates that they are about to achieve a perfect peacefulness, masterful and in possession of happiness. The poison of the serpent-lights, however, is that they never do, that every formlessness becomes another form, another containable image, another image of "the flecked animal."

The dissolving action of the second section is that of the experience of a man, a father perhaps, who used to go to a cabin on the beach as a place, a home, where he could sit by the fire and luxuriate in his colorful imaginings. Here, now, all his experience is reduced to a colorlessness, a whiteness, which itself, under the force of the auroras, is a complexity of whiteness changing to other whitenesses. The cabin itself is no longer a container; it too is caught up in the dissolving movement of the scene, is exposed and at one with the drifting waste. "The wind is blowing the sand across the floor." Even the man, who is inside and outside the cabin, which, having been turned inside-out, no longer has a distinct inside and outside, even the man has ceased to be self-contained, has ceased to be distinguishable from what he observes, as he "turns blankly on the sand." His blankness is at one with his observation of

> how the north is always enlarging the change,
> With its frigid brilliances, its blue-red sweeps,
> And gusts of great enkindlings, its polar-green,
> The color of ice and fire and solitude.
>
> (II. pp. 412-13)

He has become one with the forms gulping after formlessness, is himself such a form, an individual man going through the process of dissolution, becoming formless, and yet always a form becoming formless. There will and will not be a return to him, in the skyey father of sections IV and V, and in the scholar of section VI, who experiences the dissolution of "the frame / Of everything he is," as he beholds "An arctic effulgence flaring" on it and as he feels afraid. And, of course, the form of that scholar will immediately dissolve, in section VII, into a masculine imagination "that sits enthroned / As grim as it is benevolent," "sitting / In highest night."

In section III the mother goes through the same process as the man did in the previous section. She is the purpose of the poem, the satisfaction that will suffice, the interior paramour whose gentle affection makes a poem all interior, all contained, with everything that is interior transparent to every other thing. But the intimacy of interiority is dissolved under the auroras of autumn. The mother's necklace is not experienced as part of a kiss; it becomes hard, observed from outside, a carving. Likewise, her soft hands cease to be a touch, part of the intimate darkness, and become a mere motion. "The house will crumble"; all sense of innerness is destroyed. Yet even as this dissolution occurs, a vaster innerness appears; all is dissolved, yet, beyond the dissolution, there is a shelter in which all are at ease, the shelter of the mind, the container of containers, at one with the lights of the vast sky. The mother falls asleep, she does not die. Her dissolution is the folding over of the house, so that what was inner becomes outer, but the outerness is part of a vaster innerness, an innerness contained by the houseless house of the lights flashing and fading away. At one with this vastness, we look back upon the original house as something that has been emptied; there is no light within it. The only light comes from outside it, so that the windows alone, not the rooms, are illuminated. The command has been issued by the north wind, the house abandoned, and all have become one with that naked wind which spreads its windy grandeurs round. The only action is exterior to the house, as is the wind's knocking "like a rifle-butt against the door."

For all this destruction, the mother will reappear as the dark softness of the vaster house of the skies. In section V she will invite "humanity to her house / And table," though the festival celebrated there will lack the intimacy that was lost in section III; it will be a tumult, a "loud, disordered mooch." In sections VIII and IX, she will appear again as the true purpose of this poem, as the vast darkness at one with the flashing of the lights in the sky, as if she were "the innocent mother" who "sang in the dark / Of the room and on an accordian, half heard, / Created the time and place in which we breathed . . ." Like the man of section II, then, she is "form gulping after formlessness" which at once becomes another "form gulping after formlessness."

"The Auroras of Autumn" does not require sustained analysis in the way many of Stevens's poems do, primarily because it is integral not only in its depths but also on its surfaces. Once the reader has caught its basic movement, he should be able to move with it to the very end. The crucial need is to sustain the sense of the auroras of autumn, of their peculiar flashing and fading into darkness only to flash as fading into darkness again. In section IV, for example, it is this visual image which animates the father's "no to no" and "yes to yes" and "yes to no." It is a saying farewell that recurs and recurs. Further, it is the auroras themselves which explain why the father is no longer leaping "from heaven to heaven more rapidly / Than bad angels leap from heaven to hell in flames." In earlier poems, the movement of the surface of Stevens's imagination is discontinuous; one's head is rocked again and again as he is forced to leap from one world of imagery to another. Here, however, the father "sits in quiet and green-a-day." The ever-changingness of the imagination has at last found a visual image which is contained; the movement of lights into darkness and lights into darkness, the very essence of the poetic action in so many of Stevens's finest poems, is here realized visually within the single image of the auroras of autumn.

The problem of the remaining sections of the poem, a problem which gradually dissolves, is the understanding of how these lights can be experienced as pure innocence. For all their transiency, they are still lights, shapes, containers; they are the masks of the father's actors who perform this marvelous festival of lights. How, then, can they "choir it with the naked wind"? How can they be utterly at one with pure nakedness and innocence? Only, it seems, by realizations of these images as identical with non-images, of lights at one with darkness. Thus, in section V the musicians are dubbing at a tragedy which is not really a tragedy, since "there are no lines to speak," "There is no play." Section VI, which is surely the visual climax of the poem, presents the display in the sky as a theater floating through the clouds which is really not a theater but itself another cloud, although it has a definiteness and substance which the other clouds lack, being "of misted rock / And mountains running like water, wave on wave, / Through waves of light." The peril of this section lies in its tendency to fix this superb display of "form gulping after formlessness" as a definite, realized form, a form which one fixes with the name of the auroras of autumn. Even though its form is a violation of our conventional notions of form, so that the denouement is repeatedly postponed, it is undoubtedly acquiring a form of repeated movement. Thus, Stevens breaks beyond our pleasure in the fixity of naming with

> This is nothing until in a single man contained,
> Nothing until this named thing nameless is
> And is destroyed.
>
> (VI. p. 416)

The sense of the auroras as a vision thus breaks down as we are moved beyond it to a higher action, to the action of a man containing the image within himself and sensing, in its dissolving process, the imminence of his own dissolution.

Section VII extends this development to unfix the fixity of "form gulping after formlessness." From the image of the scholar Stevens moves to the image of a supreme imagination which is sitting in the north and, as "the white creator of black," is extinguishing everything except the symbols of extinguishing, the "crown and mystical cabala" of the aurora borealis. If, however, this supreme imagination, these lights flashing into darkness, were destiny, then it could not leap by chance into utter annihilation without violating its own law. "It must change from destiny to slight caprice," its very law must become lawlessness, capriciousness, so that it contains as part of its supremacy the chance of its own dissolution, a dissolution which would result from "a flippant communication under the moon," a harrowing retreat into the "shivering residue" of a man in his denial of the magnificence of the imagination.

By way of this complication, Stevens is now ready to affirm a faith in innocence as identical with the anticipation of disaster. The movement of the lights is at one with the nothingness of the darkness into which they move, and the sense that

by slight caprice, by a flippant communication under the
moon, by the speaking of "the simplest word," the whole festival may be annihilated, becomes "the tenderest and the truest
part" of the innocence of the lights. So long as the fatherly
lights continue to flash, the dark into which they go is the
innocent mother, is death as the mother of beauty. Only,
however, after one has imagined the mother as utter annihilation, as sheer formlessness, can the flashing lights, the eyes
that open and fix on us in every sky, be the seeing of a being
that is beyond any and all limited perspectives. Only at the
very point in time when the lights of even the stars seem like
"the last embellishment" of the "great shadow" of nothingness, only then, with the sense of disaster as imminent, with a
flippant word about to be spoken, only then do we experience
the rendezvous with the mother in its perfect freedom and
feel as though we are "hale-hearted landsmen," "Danes in
Denmark all day long."

After the experience of innocence as full of the imminence
of disaster, in sections VIII and IX, there is nowhere to go
except into annihilation itself, and thus the last section is
spoken out of pure blankness. We are beyond the vastness
of the imagination that contains life and death, being and
nothingness, father and mother, and even a sense of their
annihilation within itself. We are, in other words, in a state
of annihilation, and thus the words plod along in the last
section without imaginative resonance. This is a coda to the
poem, and is a coldness beyond all sense of coldness. It is not
the absence of the imagination imagined; it is, as flatly as it
can be, the absence of the imagination. It is not like free
verse so close to metered verse that it can be felt as denying
it; it is like free verse presented frankly as so far beyond meter
that it denies even its link of denial with it. Accomplished
within the action of the whole poem, however, it can be felt
as effectively blank. "An unhappy people in a happy world."
We look back on the poem as the oneness of "unhappy peo-

ple" and "a happy world," and our happiness in this reflection is the dry emptiness of annihilation. Even here, however,
after all the dry abstractions concerning "the spectre of the
spheres," there is a turning back toward imaginative life, and
a renewal of our faith in "The vital, the never-failing genius,"
as the concluding lines re-evoke the auroral lights:

> by these lights
> Like a blaze of summer straw, in winter's nick.

There is always a nick, an incision, in the deepest, coldest state
of wintriness through which an imaginative light may flash
"Like a blaze of summer straw." And the rest is darkness. No
other poem ends with such finality as this one, because it contains that which extends beyond it within itself. The flippant
word has been spoken, by slight caprice, before the beginning
of section X. The emptiness and blankness that extend beyond
the last lines of the poem, this abstract death among rabbis
has been realized within this concluding section of the poem
itself. No poet has come closer to writing out of the blank
happiness of death itself in such a way as to make that terrible banality function as part of a genuine poem. If this
sounds unduly ingenious, it is my fault, not Stevens's. For that
matter, Stevens often lures his critic to stretch his mind beyond its capacity even into the arid zones of mere ingenuity.
Even in those zones, however, the poem of which the critic
speaks may blaze up, momentarily.

IV

If "The Auroras of Autumn" is for me the truly great poem
of this last period of Stevens's career, it is necessary to say that
"An Ordinary Evening in New Haven" might well appear to
be even greater to an elderly reader.[17] Of this, his longest
poem, Stevens said: "This longer poem may seem diffuse and

casual."[18] The poem may seem diffuse and rambling, but Stevens knew it was not. It is rather the supremely delicate articulation of the garrulousness of old age. Each of its thirty-one sections is composed as "an and yet, and yet, and yet." In fact, the impression is that the poet simply cannot stop talking. Even the ending lacks finality and seems to be no more than a pause:

> It is not in the premise that reality
> Is a solid. It may be a shade that traverses
> A dust, a force that traverses a shade.
>
> (XXXI. p. 489)

Or a something that traverses a something and on and on. The voice falters weakly, more weakly than in any other stanza of the entire poem. Perhaps the poet has dozed off; one feels that when he rouses himself, he will go on as before, with more and more "and yets."

The poet, however, has a purpose beyond mere talking. As he said himself: "my interest is to try to get as close to the ordinary, the commonplace and the ugly as it is possible for a poet to get. It is not a question of grim reality but of plain reality. The object is of course to purge oneself of anything false."[19]

> The eye's plain version is a thing apart,
> The vulgate of experience. Of this
> A few words, an and yet, and yet, and yet—
>
> (I. p. 465)

All the extraordinary intricacy of this garrulous voice has as its purpose the saying of a few things about its very opposite, the ordinary, the commonplace. The poem, as must be obvious to every reader, is by no means purged of everything false. It is rather the act of purging oneself of everything false. Instead of "The poem of pure reality," it is a poem in which

We seek

The poem of pure reality, untouched
By trope or deviation, straight to the word,
Straight to the transfixing object, to the object

At the exactest point at which it is itself,
Transfixing by being purely what it is,
A view of New Haven, say, through the certain eye,

The eye made clear of uncertainty, with the sight
Of simple seeing, without reflection.

(IX. p. 471)

No poem by Stevens is fuller of reflection, of yet another "and yet, and yet, and yet." Though not the poem of pure reality, it is a poem in which Stevens seeks for the poem of pure reality; and, strikingly enough, it is also a poem in which he discovers the poem of pure reality. The whole impure poem moves to its climax in the purity of purities of its thirtieth section:

The last leaf that is going to fall has fallen.
The robins are là-bas, the squirrels, in tree-caves,
Huddle together in the knowledge of squirrels.

The wind has blown the silence of summer away.
It buzzes beyond the horizon or in the ground:
In mud under ponds, where the sky used to be reflected.

The barrenness that appears is an exposing.
It is not part of what is absent, a halt
For farewells, a sad hanging on for remembrances.

It is a coming on and a coming forth.
The pines that were fans and fragrances emerge,
Staked solidly in a gusty grappling with rocks.

The glass of the air becomes an element—
It was something imagined that has been washed away.
A clearness has returned. It stands restored.

197

It is not an empty clearness, a bottomless sight.
It is a visibility of thought,
In which hundreds of eyes, in one mind, see at once.
                                        (XXX. pp. 487-88)

This section, and this section alone, realizes pure ordinariness, barrenness being exposed, and it is the purity which the whole poem has moved to create. After the reader has recreated the scene in its barrenness, moreover, he finds that the existence of that barrenness is composed almost wholly of the nonexistence of its opposite, that the essential Is-ness of the section is the immediate identity of Is and Is-not. The eye's plain version is minimal: there is the horizon, the ground, and the ponds, pines that emerge "Staked solidly in a gusty grappling with rocks" and "The glass of the air" that has become "an element." There is nothing else; that is, there is the nothing of all the things that compose the Is-not of the scene: the falling leaves, the robins and squirrels, the silence of summer and the wind that blew it away; the buzzing of a wind inaudible but imaginable, the mud asserted but unseen, the reflective ponds that are not, the pines that are not fans and fragrances.

To behold the eye's plain version, one must have an experience "In which hundreds of eyes, in one mind, see at once." One must look blankly on the sand and at the same moment see with "eyes that open and fix on us in every sky." To experience the savagery of plainness, one must be aware of all the intricacies that are excluded by the plainness. To capture the sense of bare rock, one must sense the shadow of otherness, of its converse that, as unreal, invisible, absent, false, is as much a part of his sense of the plainness as the rock itself is. "Real and unreal are two in one." A person can experience New Haven as it is, when he is actually in its presence, only if at the same time he feels the sense he had of it before he arrived. The barrenness of the scene evoked in the thirtieth

198

section is manifest only to him who realizes, as part of it, all the vitality and beauty and intricacy that was once present, but is no longer. The clearness of the plain scene is not empty or bottomless; it is a clearness seen by one who brings to bear upon the scene all the invisibility of his desire, not as memory but as the Is-not of the scene. "The point of vision and desire are the same." To see plainly one must see with "desire, set deep in the eye, / Behind all actual seeing, in the actual scene." The full awareness of the section, then, is an experience in which "as and is are one," in which grim reality and paradisal parlance, in which "the life of the world" and the "words of the world," in which the real and the unreal are beyond either fact or fancy, taken in themselves, in an utter oneness. Plainness and the garrulousness of old age are thus an identity like that of actual Rome and celestial Rome or that of innocence and disaster.

So utterly at one are the real and unreal of "An Ordinary Evening" that Stevens can, in the thirty-first section, reverse their relationship without disruption. In the end, the invisible and intricate and insubstantial are presented as reality at one with the visible and plain and solid as unreality. The emphasis of the final section is not on sounds, but on their "less legible meanings," on

> the little reds
> Not often realized, the lighter words
> In the heavy drum of speech, the inner men
>
> Behind the outer shields, the sheets of music
> In the strokes of thunder, dead candles at the window
> When day comes, fire-foams in the motions of the sea
> (XXXI. p. 488)

The final form, the ultimate reality, of this vast, shadowy poem is to be found in the

199

Flickings from finikin to fine finikin
And the general fidget from busts of Constantine
To photographs of the late president, Mr. Blank

The venerable mask that is the actual present of agedness, "The poem of the mind in the act of finding / What will suffice," the unreal ruler of reality who rules what is unreal, is the paradisal parlance of "an and yet, and yet, and yet" spoken of "grim reality," of "The eye's plain version," "The vulgate of experience." Nonetheless, if this unreal speech is ultimate reality, if it is "the edgings and inchings of final form," it always moves from and to and about the commonplace, with which it is finally identical. If it is a shade, it traverses a dust; if a force, it traverses a shade.

For all his concern with metamorphosis, transiency, and the most subtle nuance, Stevens does not, even in so mysterious and subjective a poem as this, let go of the common and solid and ordinary. To give oneself up to constant change, to neglect "morning and evening" as "like promises kept," and "the approaching sun and its arrival, / Its evening feast and the following festival," such paradisal parlance, dissociated from grim reality, was never a temptation for Stevens. Even at the extreme point of age, where he felt the "radial aspect of this place" to have its source in a figure like Ecclesiast, for whom all is vanity, Stevens maintained "a faithfulness as against the lunar light." Even as at one with hundreds of eyes, as "a citizen of heaven," even when he seemed to escape his own will and "in his nakedness / Inhabit the hypnosis" of a celestial sphere, even at the extreme of aged dissolution, Stevens remained faithful to life itself, to that "permanent, abstract" hidalgo, who is "A hatching that stared and demanded an answering look." He "kept coming back and coming back to the real."

As an ordinary evening itself, "An Ordinary Evening in New Haven" is one more poem as evening in a long tradition of poems as evening. As evening, the poem is an experience

200

of dissolution, of lights passing into darkness, of sharpness
dissolving into vagueness. Unlike ordinary evening poems,
however, this poem is realized as an ordinary evening. As the
poem progresses, the poet again and again begins with something ordinary, something commonplace, some simple thing
flatly stated, and then dissolves it into the intricacy and dimness and mysteriousness of evening, as the passage of plain
light into phantasmal darkness. Most of the sections, for that
matter, begin with a short and strong declaration: "The point
of vision and desire are the same"; "The plainness of plain
things is savagery"; "Reality is the beginning not the end";
"We fling ourselves, constantly longing, on this form"; "It is
fatal in the moon and empty there"; "The poem is the cry of
its occasion"; and so forth. In section after section, Stevens
returns to this syntactical form of ordinariness, as he returns,
experientially, to something as ordinary as "a hotel instead
of the hymns / That fall upon it out of the wind."

Having made this return to ordinariness, however, Stevens
repeatedly falls upon it voraciously with the most intricate,
polyphantic hymns. One look at the commonplace and it at
once becomes "a rumpling of blazons," as the real turns into
something most unreal. As this progression occurs and recurs,
moreover, one realizes that he is moving, and has been moving all along, to a triumphant identification of the common
and the extraordinary, of the barren and the fecund.

> This endlessly elaborating poem
> Displays the theory of poetry,
> As the life of poetry. A more severe,
>
> More harassing master would extemporize
> Subtler, more urgent proof that the theory
> Of poetry is the theory of life,
>
> As it is, in the intricate evasions of as,
> In things seen and unseen, created from nothingness,
> The heavens, the hells, the worlds, the longed-for lands.
>
> (XXVIII. p. 486)

201

What the poet is willing to say is that the ideas in poetry, the intricate, articulatory movements of the poet's thinking, are truly identical with the life of poetry, with the inner impulsion of feeling that is the source and motive of the poetry. Poetry, that is, is self-translation. The articulation of the poem is a translation of its elemental feeling, but there is no elemental feeling without the articulation of it; thus the translation is a translation of itself; in reality, desire and vision are the same, feeling and image are identical. This is real. This the poet believes, that "Real and unreal are two in one" in poetry. The poet himself will not say "that the theory / Of poetry is the theory of life." But he does say that "A more severe, / More harassing master" would say this and give proof of it. The theory of poetry is the life of poetry is the theory of life. Presumably, the next words would be that these are all, finally, identical with life itself. This claim would be the unreality set against the reality of the poem, with all its reality and unreality contained within it. Could this poet, could any poet, say so much? As an old man on the verge of death, it seems that Stevens can.

> Our breath is like a desperate element
> That we must calm, the origin of a mother tongue
>
> With which to speak to her, the capable
> In the midst of foreignness, the syllable
> Of recognition, avowal, impassioned cry,
>
> The cry that contains its converse in itself,
> In which looks and feelings mingle and are part
> As a quick answer modifies a question,
>
> Not wholly spoken in a conversation between
> Two bodies disembodied in their talk,
> Too fragile, too immediate for any speech.
>
> (VIII. pp. 470-71)

At the end of life there is an identification of our breath and the most subtle conversation that is our poetry. Life itself becomes disembodied at such a time and is fully realized only as poetry, as this kind of talk, which is "Too fragile, too immediate for any speech." Perhaps the full experience of such a poem must be postponed until the reader himself is that

> twisted, stooping, polymathic Z,
> He that kneels always on the edge of space
>
> In the pallid perceptions of its distances.
> (VI. p. 469)

Only then will the look with which he answers the stare, the plain stare, of the hidalgo of life be truly the seeing of "hundreds of eyes, in one mind," hundreds of "and yet, and yet, and yets." Only then will he be able to look upon ordinary New Haven as

> an impalpable town, full of
> Impalpable bells, transparencies of sound,
>
> Sounding in transparent dwellings of the self,
> Impalpable habitations that seem to move
> In the movement of the colors of the mind,
>
> The far-fire flowing and the dim-coned bells
> Coming together in a sense in which we are poised,
> Without regard to time or where we are
> (II. p. 466)

in such a way that the town is "So much ourselves, we cannot tell apart / The idea and the bearer-being of the idea." And only then will he be able to feel the identity of the plain town and this supernally imagined town. Only then will he be able to be so mysteriously subjective and yet affirm of an old philosopher that "The life of the city never lets go, nor do you / Ever want it to."

Stevens in any case, even when on the edge of space, never looked away from life, from ordinary life, in order to sing celestial hymns. His hymns always fell upon ordinary and common experience. But how uncommon the commonness of aging and dying is, in these last poems. The marvel is that in such fidelity to common life, Stevens was able to articulate such magnificence. At the beginning of his career he composed a magnificent memorial, in "The Death of a Soldier," to all those men whom one thinks of as dying without memorial. At the end of his career, he has composed a memorial of comparable magnificence which is itself the movement of the mind of an extraordinary and common man dying a magnificently common death.

The serenity of "An Ordinary Evening in New Haven" reveals a spiritual health and fullness of being beyond our wildest imaginings of the experience of old age. The poem is imitative of nothing actual or possible. It is "A recent imagining of reality" which lifts us beyond the remotest dreams we had previously associated with human existence. Neither this poem nor the other fine poems of the end of Stevens's life should be taken as the end of a tradition of American poetry, Adamic or otherwise. These last poems of Stevens are rather a lure into the future, into a fuller and richer life than we ever before guessed at. And they can serve as the symbol and promise of a poetry even more magnificent and faithful to life than they themselves are. "Shall our blood fail?" On the crest of these poems, these "mountains running like water, wave on wave, / Through waves of light," we cannot believe it. To have been so close to death and yet so vital, so barren and yet so fecund, so plain and yet so paradisal; to have the one, in all its ruinousness, who can imagine survival without a search for the other?

Postscript

In the early 1950s, when the greatness of Stevens's poetry first burst upon large numbers of young poets and students of poetry, their response was anything but impressive. The poets were able to imitate Stevens's sophistication and the intricacies of his syntax, but not the capaciousness and the sweeping magnitudes of his best poems. Far more as a result of this than of any misplaced devotion to the New Critical notion of the complexity of all genuine poetry, much poetry of the fifties was stillborn, its syntactical complexities civilized but lifeless. By the end of the decade it seemed likely that, in order to find their own true voices, poets like Robert Bly, Galway Kinnell, W. S. Merwin, Charles Tomlinson, and James Wright were being forced to abandon civilization and retreat into some subculture, into some oriental state of passivity, or into nature, to contemplate the farmlands of Minnesota or the mountains of New England or the Far West.

During the past ten years, however, the work of these poets

has revealed that such projected retreats were largely metaphorical. In order to explore their selves more deeply, they
did have to turn away from the civilized surfaces of poetry like
Stevens's. Having made such retreats, however, having tapped
that *vis interna naturae* in the only possible way, in ways that
were their own and not Stevens's,—or Williams's or Roethke's
—they have returned to articulateness and are writing poems
both forceful and intricate, not similar to those of Stevens's,
but of comparable value. Great poems are inimitable, if imitation is thought of as direct and immediate. If influence is
either direct or absent, then the poets were obligated to kill
off their father. As Stevens knew, however, fruitful influences
and imitations must be profoundly indirect. The finest poetry
being written today proves, in my opinion, that Stevens's
poetry was not the decisive end of a long tradition of American poetry. If it was culminative, it was also originative. Imitation, Longinus was the first to explain, is either a fault or
the imitation of the excellence of other poetry; great poems
are imitative of great poems because they flow out of their own
creative fount, because they are self-originative. Imitation of
Stevens during the fifties was servile. There had to be a moment of revulsion and rejection before poets could return to
Stevens and imitate him, as they are now doing, with the
originality and independence which are the essence of all
genuine imitation.

The impact of Stevens's poems on students of poetry in
the fifties left them in a state of stunned awe. If pressed to
make a statement on one of his poems, and aware of the inadequacy of dry, analytical commentary, the student could
only remain in silence, limp off into the woods to contemplate violets or read Zen, or immerse himself in an alien
aesthetic culture, like that of Italy, seemingly irrelevant to
the magnificence of Stevens's poems. Like the poets of this
generation, its critics, having made their retreats, are now
making their returns. It is fair, I think, to say that they too

have overcome their servile adoration of Stevens and are finding ways to imitate him critically, with methods which have some of the spaciousness of Stevens's own poetry.

As a slight modification of a conviction of F. R. Leavis's, I would say that in order to sense the immediacy and vitality of great poetry of the past, in order to respond to it as contemporaneous with oneself, one must be responsive to the finest poetry that is literally contemporaneous with him. If no fine poetry were being written today, it is unlikely that critics could sense the vividness of Stevens's poems or discuss it with the needed breadth and sharpness. If critics today are manifesting any such strengths, one of their main debts must be to those poets whose achievements during the past ten years have revitalized the sense of the profundity and rarity of poetry and the sense of the poem as act as one of the ultimately real forms of human activity.

Notes

CHAPTER 1

1. René Wellek and Austin Warren, *Theory of Literature* (New York: Harcourt Brace & Co., 1949), p. 141.

2. (New York: New Directions, 1947), p. 247.

3. For a fuller exposition of this theory, see my *Neo-Idealistic Aesthetics: Croce-Gentile-Collingwood* (Detroit: Wayne State University Press, 1966), chap. 5: "Gentile's Mature Aesthetics: Art as Self-Translation."

4. For the development of this point, see Guido de Ruggiero, *Filosofi del novecento* (Bari: Laterza, 1958), pp. 318-21.

5. *Literary Essays of Ezra Pound,* ed. T. S. Eliot (New York: New Directions, 1954), p. 49.

6. See Giovanni Gentile, *Teoria generale dello spirito come atto puro* (Florence: Sansoni, 1944), pp. 19-21.

7. (Milan: Feltrinelli, 1962), pp. 185-221.

8. "Examples of Wallace Stevens," in his *Form and Value in Modern Poetry* (Garden City, N. Y.: Doubleday & Co., Inc., 1957); and "The Substance That Prevails," in *The Kenyon Review* 17 (Winter 1955): 94-110.

9. William Empson, "Wit in the *Essay on Criticism*," in his *The Structure of Complex Words* (New York: New Directions, n.d.), pp. 84-100.

10. Murray Krieger, *The Tragic Vision* (New York: Holt, Rinehart & Winston, Inc., 1960), p. 233.

11. See Karl Vossler, *The Spirit of Language in Civilization* (London: K. Paul, Trench, Trubner & Co., Ltd., 1931).

12. *Poetry and the Age* (New York: Alfred A. Knopf, 1953), p. 140.

13. *Wallace Stevens, Collected Poems* (New York: Alfred A. Knopf, 1965), p. 326.

14. Louis L. Martz, "Wallace Stevens: The World as Meditation," in *Literature and Belief*, English Institute Essays (1957), pp. 139-66.

15. *The Shaping Spirit* (London: Chatto & Windus, 1958), p. 132.

16. *Collected Poems*, p. 293.

17. On this point Richards never deviates from the position set forth in his *Principles of Literary Criticism*. For the full complexity of Pearce's position, see his *The Continuity of America Poetry* (Princeton: Princeton University Press, 1961), especially pp. 6, 302, 380-93.

18. *Letters of Wallace Stevens*, ed. Holly Stevens (New York: Alfred A. Knopf, 1966), p. 359.

19. *Collected Poems*, p. 171.

20. Ibid., p. 515.

21. "Final Soliloquy of the Interior Paramour," ibid., p. 524.

CHAPTER 2

1. Joseph N. Riddel, *The Clairvoyant Eye: The Poetry and Poetics of Wallace Stevens* (Baton Rouge: Louisiana State University Press, 1965), p. 4.

2. *Collected Poems*, pp. 91, 325.

3. Northrop Frye, "The Realistic Oriole: A Study of Wallace Stevens," *Fables of Identity* (New York: Harcourt, Brace & World, Inc., 1963), p. 247.

4. *Letters*, p. 206.

5. *Itinéraire français* (Paris, 1943), pp. 9-10; my translation:

Il me semble parfois que les vrais chefs-d'oeuvre sont des Phénix qui ont besoin de l'attention du lecteur pour renaître à chaque fois. Les autres, au contraire, les mauvais livres, se rappellent impérieusement à vous. . . . Il faut du temps, de la détente, de l'énergie pour faire revivre un chef-d'oeuvre, parce qu'un chef-d'oeuvre est justement une oeuvre d'où l'on a retiré tous ses accroche-sens et tous ses accroche-coeur. Un chef-d'oeuvre n'apparaît qu'à celui qui, sachant le lire, a déjà merité sa complicité. C'est la moins democratique des productions humaines.

6. *Complete Poems of Robert Frost, 1949* (New York: Henry Holt & Co., 1949), p. 332.
7. *Collected Poems,* p. 97.
8. *L'Allegria* (Verona: Arnoldo Mondadori, 1942), p. 104. My translation: "Soldiers. They are like/ The leaves/ On the trees/ Of autumn."
9. *Letters,* p. 251.
10. *Collected Poems,* p. 8.
11. *Introduction to Wallace Stevens* (Bloomington: Indiana University Press, 1964), p. 164.
12. *Collected Poems,* p. 55.
13. *Form and Value in Modern Poetry,* p. 185.
14. *Collected Poems,* p. 71.
15. Riddel, p. 188.
16. *Collected Poems,* pp. 15-16.
17. *Letters,* p. 464; *Collected Poems,* p. 323.
18. *Collected Poems,* p. 79.
19. Ibid., p. 78.
20. *Letters,* pp. 294, 351.
21. *Collected Poems,* p. 29.
22. Ibid., p. 45.
23. Ibid., p. 27.
24. *Letters,* p. 230.

CHAPTER 3
1. "Wallace Stevens, or the Hedonist's Progress," in *On Modern Poets* (Cleveland: The World Publishing Co., 1959), pp. 18 ff.
2. *Collected Poems,* p. 24.
3. Ibid., p. 193.
4. Ibid., p. 128.
5. Ibid., p. 239.
6. *Messages: Literary Essays* (Port Washington, N. Y.: Kennikat Press, 1964), pp. 50-51.
7. *Collected Poems,* p. 201.
8. Ibid., p. 326.
9. Ibid., p. 196.
10. See particularly, Frank Doggett, *Stevens' Poetry of Thought* (Baltimore: The Johns Hopkins Press, 1966).
11. *Collected Poems,* p. 250.
12. "Dialogue with the Audience," *Saturday Review,* November 22, 1958, pp. 10 ff.

13. *Paradiso* 26, 103-108. This is translated by Louis Biancolli in *The Divine Comedy, III, Paradise* (New York: Washington Square Press, 1966):

> Without your avowing it
> To me, I can discern your wish better
> Than you can discern whatever is most certain to you—
> Because I see it in the truthful mirror
> Which makes itself the likeness of all things,
> While nothing is the likeness of itself.

14. Jarrell, *Poetry and the Age*, p. 145.
15. *The Principles of Art* (Oxford: Oxford University Press, 1938), pp. 217, 282-85.

CHAPTER 4
1. *Letters*, p. 301.
2. *Collected Poems*, p. 126.
3. Ibid., p. 158.
4. Ibid., p. 157.
5. Ibid., p. 155.
6. *Letters*, p. 352.
7. *Opus Posthumous*, ed. Samuel French Morse (New York, 1957), p. 48.
8. Ibid., p. 71.
9. On the dust jacket of *The Man with the Blue Guitar and Other Poems* (New York: Alfred A. Knopf, 1937).
10. Riddel, *The Clairvoyant Eye*, pp. 136, 138.
11. *Letters*, Aug. 8, 1940, p. 359.
12. "Concordia Discors in the Poetry of Wallace Stevens," *American Literature* 34 (May 1962): 254-62.
13. *Letters*, p. 359.
14. Ibid., pp. 289, 292, 295.

CHAPTER 5
1. Glauco Cambon, "Wallace Stevens: 'Notes toward a Supreme Fiction,'" in his *The Inclusive Flame* (Bloomington: Indiana University Press, 1963); Doggett, pp. 98-115; Riddel, pp. 165-85; Ronald Sukenick, *Wallace Stevens: Musing the Obscure* (New York: New York University Press, 1967), pp. 136-62, among others.
2. *Letters*, p. 359.
3. "Concordia Discors."
4. See especially "Imagination as Value," *The Necessary Angel* (New York: Alfred A. Knopf, 1951).

5. *Purgatorio* 24. "I am one who, when love breathes in one, take note, and in that manner which he dictates within go on to set it forth." Translated by John D. Sinclair in *Dante's Purgatorio* (New York: Oxford University Press, 1961).

6. See, as examples, the essays on Stevens in A. Alvarez, *The Shaping Spirit* (London, 1958); George S. Fraser, *Vision and Rhetoric* (London: Faber & Faber, 1959); and M. J. Collie, "The Rhetoric of Accurate Speech," *Essays in Criticism* 12 (Jan. 1962): 54-66. The same could not be said of Frank Kermode, *Wallace Stevens* (Edinburgh: Oliver & Boyd, 1960).

7. Jarrell, p. 142. Shapiro, *In Defence of Ignorance* (New York: Random House, 1960), p. 245.

8. *Forms of Discovery* ([Denver]: Alan Swallow, 1967), p. 277.

9. The exceptions I think of are Mario Fubini, *Metrica e poesia,* and Harvey Gross, *Sound and Form in Modern Poetry* (Ann Arbor: University of Michigan Press, 1964).

CHAPTER 6

1. For this clash, see Joseph Riddel, "The Contours of Stevens Criticism," *The Act of the Mind,* ed. Roy Harvey Pearce and J. Hillis Miller (Baltimore: Johns Hopkins Press, 1965).

2. *Collected Poems,* p. 241.

3. Ibid., p. 250.

4. For "La Ginestra," see Leopardi's *Canti,* ed. Mario Fubini (Turin: Loescher, 1964) or Edwin Morgan's translation, "The Broom," in Leopardi, *Poems and Prose,* ed. Angel Flores (Bloomington: Indiana University Press, 1966).

5. For the finest studies of the recent past, see Giovanni Gentile, *Manzone e Leopardi* (Milan: Treves, 1928), chap. 3, "Introduzione a Leopardi," and chap. 6, "La poesia del Leopardi"; and Umberto Bosco, *Titanismo e pietà in Giacomo Leopardi* (Florence: F. Le Monnier, 1957).

6. As in Frederick J. Hoffman, *The Mortal No* (Princeton: Princeton University Press, 1964).

7. See Frank Lentricchia, *The Gaiety of Language: An Essay on the Radical Poetics of W. B. Yeats and Wallace Stevens* (Berkeley: University of California Press, 1968), and J. Hillis Miller, *Poets of Reality* (Cambridge: Harvard University Press, 1965). For Miller, Stevens fails to attain such a radical realism.

8. "Motives and Motifs in the Poetry of Marianne Moore," *A Grammar of Motives* (New York: Prentice-Hall, 1945), pp. 485-502.

CHAPTER 7

1. Soviet critical realism has this idea as its basis, as does the criticism of Georg Lukács.

2. For a full treatment of this idea of poetry, see Stephen Spender, *The Struggle of the Modern* (Berkeley: University of California Press, 1963).

3. Francis Fergusson, *The Idea of a Theater* (Princeton: Princeton University Press, 1949); Galvano della Volpe, *Critica del gusto* (Milan: Feltrinelli, 1960).

4. This claim is in accord with R. P. Blackmur but in opposition to Northrop Frye.

5. *Collected Poems,* p. 446.

6. Ibid., p. 66.

7. See *Forms of Discovery,* p. 368, n. 10.

8. *Letters,* p. 250.

9. *Collected Poems,* p. 368.

10. Ibid., p. 158 for the poem and p. 314 for the quotation.

11. Ibid., p. 290.

CHAPTER 8

1. See Roy Harvey Pearce, *The Continuity of American Poetry,* pp. 415, 423.

2. *Collected Poems,* p. 502.

3. Ibid., p. 509.

4. Ibid., p. 488.

5. Ibid., p. 506.

6. Ibid., p. 483.

7. Ibid., p. 472.

8. Ibid., p. 508.

9. Ibid., p. 524.

10. Ibid., p. 533.

11. This sort of thing is spread throughout the works of Kenneth Burke, but is most prominent in his most recent book, *Language as Symbolic Action* (Berkeley: University of California Press, 1966).

12. "Of Mere Being," *Opus Posthumous,* p. 117.

13. Ibid., p. 96.

14. Yvor Winters preferred "ear" to "air" (*Forms of Discovery,* pp. 367-68, n. 9), and apparently his argument for

"ear" is behind Samuel French Morse's changing "air" to "ear" in the second printing of the *Opus Posthumous*. That Winters would prefer "ear" is no surprise. Unlike Stevens, he believed in the infallibility of his bodily ear, in its final findings, just as he believed in the perfection of his eyes when judging Airedales. It should be noted, however, that Winters's preference is in accord with his belief that "The Course of a Particular" is virtually a repudiation of everything Stevens wrote after "Sunday Morning" and "The Death of a Soldier." Unfortunately, my preference for "air" is supported only by my reading of the poem, for Stevens was alive to proofread the 1951 version of the poem, but not the 1957 version. All I can factually maintain is that it is likely that Stevens recognized "air" as an alternative to "ear." I cannot believe that "air" is merely a typing error made by Stevens's secretary. The typed version of the poem which Stevens sent to *The Hudson Review*—and a copy of which Holly Stevens has graciously sent me—shows no correction from "air" to "ear." If, as seems likely, Stevens's secretary made the copy with "air" from a written version done by Stevens, I can hardly imagine her mistaking "ear" for "air." If the poem had been dictated to her, of course, that would be another matter. At worst, then, I would claim that "air" and "ear" were both in the air of Stevens's imagination. If Stevens's final finding was "ear" instead of "air," then he made a mistake, the kind he knew he was capable of, the kind Winters himself was capable of.
15. *Collected Poems*, p. 508.
16. Ibid., p. 411.
17. Ibid., p. 465.
18. *Letters*, p. 719.
19. Ibid., p. 636.

Index

216

Merle E. Brown, professor of English at the University of Iowa, received his A.B., M.A., and Ph.D. degrees from the University of Michigan. In 1966 his book Neo-Idealistic Aesthetics: Croce-Gentile-Collingwood *was published by the Wayne State University Press and in 1969 his* Kenneth Burke *appeared. He is editor of* The Iowa Review.

This manuscript was edited by Marguerite C. Wallace. The book was designed by Don Ross. The type face for the text is Linotype Baskerville originally cut by John Baskerville in the 18th century. The display face is also Baskerville.
The text is printed on Glatfelter's RR Antique paper, and the book is bound in Arkwright—Interlaken's linen cloth over binders' boards. Manufactured in the United States of America.